When God Provides

D1585439

AN OMF BOOK

© OVERSEAS MISSIONARY FELLOWSHIP
(formerly China Inland Mission)
Published by Overseas Missionary Fellowship (IHQ) Ltd.,
2 Cluny Road, Singapore 1025,
Republic of Singapore
First published 1986

OMF BOOKS are distributed by
OMF, 404 South Church Street,
Robesonia, Pa 19551, USA,
OMF, Belmont, The Vine,
Sevenoaks, Kent, TN13 3TZ, UK
OMF, PO Box 177, Kew East,
Victoria 3102, Australia
and other OMF offices.

ISBN 9971-972-44-1

Printed in Singapore.

CONTENTS

"YOU NEVER ASK FOR MONEY?"

The voice was incredulous. The speaker, a young woman in her early thirties, had until recently been a member of a radical organization working to overthrow a corrupt and unjust government. She had now been converted and was in love with the Lord Jesus, but was still bitterly critical of the smug selfishness of the established church. Through a misunderstanding, she found herself at an OMF Prayer Conference where she was like a fish out of water.

"You mean, you literally never appeal for funds? Then who pays?" she demanded. Sally was squatting on the bunkroom floor rolling up her sleeping bag. The conference was over and she was very confused by all she had seen and heard.

"The Fellowship is supported by God," OMF missionary Linnet Hinton told her and explained how, as a mission, we were committed to a policy of non-solicitation. "If God really is, then we can trust Him. If we have a need, we believe it is sufficient to tell our Lord about it and He will meet that need. The way He does so is up to Him. Sometimes He does it in very direct ways, miraculous too, like the time in the Bible when He sent birds to carry food to His hungry servant. More usually He moves by His Spirit in the hearts of other Christians to give what is needed. It's amazing how often the amount prayed for matches precisely the amount received."

"But does this really *work*?" she pleaded. "Do *you* personally know it is true?" Here was a soul searching desperately for a practical spirituality that would relate to the realities of daily living.

So Linnet shared with her some of the occasions in

3

her own life and service when God had met specific needs for money or something else through people who, humanly speaking, could not possibly have known about them. She explained how, without any solicitation, God had supplied the material needs of the Overseas Missionary Fellowship (formerly known as the China Inland Mission) for over a hundred years, and that as the size and scope of the work had increased, so also had His supply, until the previous year the amount received had been eight million dollars!

Sally had been particularly impressed, Linnet discovered, with the quality of life displayed by some of our retired OMF colleagues at the conference. There was an infectious joyousness and vitality about them that was almost youthful; a serenity and confidence that stood in marked contrast to the anxiety, fear and insecurity that often characterizes the elderly. Yet few of them owned their own homes or had more than enough to cover current needs. They were living demonstrations that it is no vain thing to trust the living God.

That particular generation of missionaries had served the Lord through the tumultuous days of the Sino-Japanese War and the subsequent Communist victory in China. Time and again they had been thrown into utter dependence upon the Lord for the basic necessities of life, and even for life itself. After leaving China many of them, in their middle years, had had to start all over again in other countries, to learn new languages, adapt to new cultures and adjust to the trials of a tropical climate. And through it all they had proved abundantly that God can be trusted.

"But who supports them now?" Sally wanted to know.

"There is no old-age pension for them in this

country, so they still share in the income of the Fellowship and live by the faith that has governed their whole lives."

"Then it's true. By God it's true!" she said reverently. "This is the reality I've been looking for all my life. When I became a Christian, I gave up my job because it was the sort of job a Christian can't do. I am now unemployed and the only thing I own is the car in which I came to this conference. I've been anxious and afraid. I've been disillusioned with the church and have despised the hypocrisy of many Christians who are so materialistic and complacent in spite of the poverty of others. But you have shown me that the life of faith works and that God can be trusted, and so, I too, from this day on, want to depend upon Him alone for all my needs."

Linnet Hinton, who shared this testimony with me, is herself a person living by the same principles. She knows they work. Jesus once asked His disciples a question on the same subject. "When I sent you without purse, bag, or sandals, did you lack anything?" "Nothing," they answered. When God provides, people need not fear to lose out. His provision may sometimes be simple, but it is enough.

This book is not really about money. It is about God and his faithfulness. Money itself is neutral, and there are many ways of obtaining it, some good, some bad; but when we die we leave it all behind anyway. Whether God exists or not is a much more important issue; and if He exists, can He be trusted? The answer to these questions affects our whole lives, and our life after death.

We who have been involved in the stories in this book, and in the life of the China Inland Mission and Overseas Missionary Fellowship, begin from a position of faith. We believe God does exist. We have become convinced of this in a variety of ways, but all of us have experienced the grace of God in bringing us to know Himself through Jesus Christ and through rebirth by His Spirit. We believe we have good grounds for believing in Him through the historical fact of the resurrection of Jesus Christ from the dead: we believe that someone who said He would die and rise again, and did it, is credible in every other way. Therefore we are prepared to trust Him, not only for the eternal salvation of our souls, but also for the practical provision of our daily bread and financial support.

On one occasion Jesus said to a sick man, "Son, your sins are forgiven." Those around began to murmur and to suggest that this was blasphemy. And who could test the truth of a statement like that anyway? So Jesus took it a step further and said to them, "Why are you thinking these things? Which is easier: to say to the paralytic, 'Your sins are forgiven,' or to say, 'Get up, take your mat and walk'?" (Mark 2:8-9). Our Lord then proceeded to prove His power to operate in the unseen realm by working in the realm of the seen. In some ways, that is exactly what we want to show you in this book. We want to demonstrate that God can be trusted to do all that He says He will do, by sharing how He has provided for such mundane needs as plane tickets, meals, medical expenses, and the regular support of a whole group of Christian people for well over a hundred years.

When God provides it tells us something about His nature. We know HE IS DEPENDABLE. Our founder, Dr J Hudson Taylor, put it this way,

"There is a living God.
He has spoken in the Bible.
He means what He says
And will do all that He has promised."

Hebrews 1:1 tells us that "faith is being sure of what we hope for and certain of what we do not see." We cannot see the living God but, if He really is there, we can expect Him to keep to His word. Faith is prepared to put that to the test, and Hudson Taylor felt he had to do so before he went to China. In those days, the 1850s, there were no telephones and a letter took six months to reach China. He realized that he could well find himself with no visible means of support and no way of knowing whether anything was on the way. But he believed that God is not limited to one way of supply and is well aware of His children's needs. He believed that when Jesus told His disciples that they were of more value than many sparrows and could therefore depend upon God for the supply of their needs, He was not being super-spiritual or idealistic, but realistic.

So Hudson Taylor decided not to remind his employer about paying his salary, but simply to tell the Lord about it. The good doctor for whom he worked promptly forgot to pay him. Hudson Taylor knew that he had only to mention money and he would be paid right away, but something more important than money was at stake: would God really supply his needs and thereby prove His faithfulness to His promises? Hudson Taylor gave away his last coin to a poor family. The next day a letter came in which was enclosed some money — four times what he had shared with others the day before! But still the old doctor failed to remember. Soon this special provision from the Lord was almost gone, and the landlady was due her rent. Finally his employer remembered that he had forgotten to pay him, only to dash Hudson Taylor's expectations by saying that he had no cash available until after the weekend. He could miss a few meals, he thought, but what about the landlady waiting for her rent? Then, later that night, as he was leaving the office, the doctor ran after him. A rich patient had just arrived to pay a bill and, most uncharacteristically, had paid in cash. So Hudson Taylor went home with his salary bursting his pocket and a song of praise bursting his heart![1]

The so-called "faith principle" in missions grew from that small beginning. What we want to share with you is not that everyone has to live under this principle, but that God is still alive today and just as trustworthy as ever He was. More than money is at stake. Unfortunately, in a materialistic age, we can often provide so much ourselves that we think we do not need to trust God for anything, and then we miss out on the thrill of discovering just how real He is. Before we can honestly say that we know God is the one who has met our need, we have to go without and put ourselves in a position where no one but He can be the answer. Indeed, God sometimes puts His people in just that kind of place to prove His love. Moses, in talking to the children of Israel about their experiences in the desert, reminded them that God had "humbled you, causing you to hunger and then feeding you with manna, which neither you nor your fathers had known, to teach you that man does not live by bread alone but on every word that comes from the mouth of the Lord" (Deut. 8:3). Until they had run out of every other kind of food, the people were not ready to say that the provision had all come from God; but when they were right out of their own supplies any provision had to be from heaven, and from heaven it came. So they learned the valuable lesson that God supplies men's needs, and man must live in total dependence upon Him. Anything that teaches us that has got to be worthwhile.

When China Evangelical Seminary was established in Taiwan in 1970 the Lord taught us many such lessons of His faithfulness. Without mission boards or local churches committed to supporting this new venture in theological education for university graduates, we had only His promise and the conviction that He is completely trustworthy. "Only His promise"! What else did we need? Obedience. For ten years we did not lack. And as the staff and student body grew from twenty to one hundred, the Lord's monthly provision also increased to match the need of the growing CES family. Added to that, the Lord graciously gave the seminary a permanent home in Taipei worth more than two million dollars.

The stories in this book show that it is right not only to trust God for ourselves, but also for our dependents. John and Blodwyn Timms needed transport to the hospital for the birth of their baby; the Yips and Cheong Soh Lim were concerned about their parents, for in Chinese culture filial responsibility is extremely important. Others write of accommodation provided for the family, or medical expenses for sick wives. Each found, as Soh Lim puts it, that the consequences of our obedience are God's responsibility.

If we are to know without a doubt that God is dependable, that means WE DO NOT NEED TO TALK TO MEN ABOUT OUR NEEDS. This was a second principle on which Hudson Taylor began to act. At first, he not only trusted the Lord to supply, but also let it be widely known exactly what the needs of the Mission were. Then he began to think that people could well be influenced by what he said, rather than by God's moving them in their hearts to give, so he stopped making announcements of need. This did not mean that he was not prepared to tell people any facts they wanted to know.

Still today, OMF has no conspiracy of silence. We keep accounts and are willing to share them, and if God moves people to become involved in the work He has given us to do, we will gladly share all the financial information they would like to know. That is different from *our* moving people by *our* appeal to their interest or sympathy, where their response might be prompted by our presentation rather than by God's moving. But we believe God can be trusted, and and we are anxious lest any appeal of ours should take from Him the glory of His gracious and sufficient provision. You will find within these pages examples ranging from an OMF director deliberately keeping quiet about retired workers' needs, to parents concerned about kindergarten and school fees. A Thai Christian leader living by the same spirit of faith also experienced the joy of God's provision. We rejoice to be able to say that if God did not exist, we would have been bankrupt years ago. There is no other explanation but God!

That leads to a third principle governing the testimonies recorded in this book. We may not make appeals to men, but we are ready and willing to make our requests known to the Lord Himself. Hudson Taylor expressed it for the early pioneers of our mission by saying, "Learn to move men through God by prayer alone". This third principle is the PRINCIPLE OF PRAYER.

Paul wrote to the Philippians, "Do not be anxious

about anything, but in everything, by prayer and petition, with thanksgiving, present your requests to God. And the peace of God, which transcends all understanding, will guard your hearts and minds in Christ Jesus" (Phil. 4:6,7). Do you believe that to be true, or just a piece of pious rhetoric? The cure for worry is prayer. The Source of supply is drawn on through prayer. Sometimes we are like the Christians to whom James wrote, "You do not have, because you do not ask God" (James 4:2).

I do not want to pretend that this way of living is easy, or never tested. When funds are low and supplies are few, or when they run out altogether, the battle is joined. The enemy comes in with suggestions that this time God will let us down. History is easy to believe, because we know the answer will come by the end of the account, but when the future lies blank before us it is another matter.

Elijah, we are told, was a man who felt just as we do. He was very ordinary and very human. One day he was told to prophesy a three-year drought, and it happened. But, of course, that meant that he was involved in the drought too. So God told him to go to a ravine and drink from the little stream there; his food would come daily through the ravens. That really sounds like a story for the birds! But Elijah trusted and went. Just as he was becoming used to the strange situation, the water in the brook dried up. This time Elijah was sent to an even more difficult assignment: he had to go to a widow and her son and ask them to share their meager and dwindling supply with him. That must have seemed both unkind and callous; but in fact it not only saved Elijah's life but also that of the woman and her son. This time the provision came, not through bread from the

11

heavens, but through the stretching of the source of supply to cover the period available. I am not interested in how that happened. I do know that it did. And we have seen many cases in our history as a Fellowship when small supplies have gone much further than, humanly speaking, they should have been able to, because God is alive.

After these experiences Elijah could stand boldly on Mount Carmel and pray with a loud voice, "Answer me O Lord, answer me, so these people will know that you, O Lord, are God, and that you are turning their hearts back again" (1 Kings 18:37). He was asking God for fire, and in preparation had poured barrels of water over the sacrifice to show that if the fire came it had to be from God. When did he learn such trust? In the process of looking to God alone for his daily needs in the ravine and with the widow.

In this book you will read of times when there was no food for the next meal, no money to buy shoes or to send for missionaries' support, no buyer for a house. In each case the Lord provided in answer to prayer.

We feel that a policy of prayer for our needs draws us into close communion with God, and provides opportunities to see His glory in ways that otherwise would be hidden from our eyes.

A corollary of these principles is the one that insists that WE WILL NOT GO INTO DEBT. Borrowing money is not necessarily wrong, but it does give us power to do some things which otherwise we might not be able to do. It may also give us power to do some things we should not be trying to do. By refusing to go into debt, we believe that we allow the Lord to set His limits on our activities. If they are in line with His will, He is as capable of supplying our need before the event as

12

afterwards, so we will wait for the supply before we undertake the expense. Obviously this is not always possible when long term projects are begun, but we can ask the Lord for confirmation of His leading through the supply of our needs. Borrowing money can be a way of manipulating our environment in order to persist in our own plans. It is not always so, but we would rather avoid the possibility.

Paul instructed the Romans to honor every obligation, whether financial or in the realm of respect. He then told them, "Let no debt remain outstanding, except the continuing debt to love one another." Mike and Sue Alfieri saw the need to obey this command before beginning missionary service, and were awestruck at the way the Lord moved their mountain of debt. When the collectors of the temple tax came to Peter and asked whether Jesus was going to pay, Jesus not only told Peter to do it but sent him fishing for a particular creature that had swallowed the right amount. He confirmed the obligation and provided the means to meet it, all in the same breath.

These are principles that do work, and they do not just apply to a special group of people. We are not a particularly special group of people anyway, but we do have a very special Lord.

A further development of our philosophy of life and service is seen in the principle of POOLING OUR RESOURCES. We do each receive our own allowances, and most of us are supported at least in part by our home churches. The New Testament clearly teaches us that God means things to be that way. Yet we also believe that our commitment to a common task in evangelism calls for equal distribution of Fellowship resources, as far as that is possible. This of course happened in the wilderness, when Israel received that wonderful provision of bread from heaven. Every morning the manna came down and people went out to gather it. We read that "The Israelites did as they were told; some gathered much, some little. And when they measured it, he who gathered much did not have too much, and he who gathered little did not have too little" (Exod. 16:17). All of them were totally dependent upon God's supply, but there was an equality of distribution.

The apostles ventured on something like this in Jerusalem, to the extent that "No one claimed that any of his possessions was his own, but they shared everything they had" (Acts 4:32). We do not do exactly that, for each member has his or her own possessions, but we do share our support, place it together in one pool and then distribute those supplies as equally as possible among our membership. That means that I as the General Director receive the same amount as the newest member of the Fellowship. Some are the recipients of much more in the way of support, and others less, but those who gather much do not have a superabundance, and those who gather less are not in want, though the lack can cause problems as Roberta Fryers shares with us.

The result is fellowship, for we know that whatever our country of origin, whether we are rich or poor, and whatever our sources of supply, we all function on the same level financially and no one is advantaged in any way. This does not mean an absolute equality, for some people may still have a private income, and some may receive more personal gifts than others, but we seek to honor the spirit of this principle by surrendering some of these if they assume an undue proportion of our

14

income. Some interesting examples of this are found in chapter 5.

Someone may ask what level of living this leads to and what are our standards? We have to answer that often they are simple by comparison with those of affluent countries in the West, and luxury compared with the grinding poverty of so many people in our world today. But we have the principle of a SIMPLE LIFESTYLE as a part of our position, not because that is the way God keeps us, but because that is the way we believe we should be living anyway. We are dedicated to reaching people for our Lord Jesus Christ. The way He did it was to live at the level of ordinary people and so He was able to speak to them from a position of equality. Incarnation is God's way of communicating His love.

All of us today face the temptations of materialism. We may not believe that material things are the only real ones, but we are surrounded by an amazing array of goods to make life easy, and the commercial world screams at us that we cannot live without this or that latest gadget. In many ways, missionaries in rural areas are spared the temptations faced by our brothers and sisters in affluent countries. There are no big shops to attract us and no luxury goods to be bought — that simplifies life a great deal. Most Westerners and an increasing numbers of Asians, however, face the daily pull of materialism that complicates life considerably for the Christian.

Jesus never condemned riches as such, but He did warn about the danger of letting them take over the affections. "Where your treasure is, there your heart will be also," was His cryptic summary of the case. When the amount of our provision does not allow us to spend out on great luxuries we do not have to make too many hard decisions, but when there is plenty of money available the heart can be pulled very hard. From this point of view, therefore, the fact that the Lord provides enough for our needs but not a superabundance for luxuries gives us a definite spiritual advantage, and saves us some heart-searching decisions. A simple lifestyle is easier to accept when God is providing it than when we have the ability to do something different.

Not that the lifestyle of our members is all that low. Certainly, when our affluent friends hear what our income actually is they sometimes say to us, "But nobody could possibly live on that these days." In fact, we do, and we live very well. We may use a pedal rather than a Porsche, and eat at the hawker stalls rather than at the Hilton, but that is no hardship. And sometimes we have to confess that the Lord gives us those extras that make us feel with Paul that we have to learn to abound as well as to have enough. Paul had learned a secret in the ups and downs of economic uncertainties, the secret of being content in any and every situation, because he knew he could draw on the strength of the Lord (Phil. 4:13).

I would like to be able to tell you that all members of our Fellowship are always content in any and every situation. That would not be true. We are flesh and blood, and sometimes our hearts get rocked when we see our contemporaries owning their own houses and cars, and even boats and swimming pools. We can become jealous of others who receive a few more personal gifts than we do, and we can begin to look at the gods of materialism as easily as anyone else. But when we come to our senses, we thank our heavenly

Father who knows just how much we do need and gives accordingly.

That, after all, is what the Christian life is all about. As believers in God, we believe that He made the world and all that is in it, and that He has set the pattern for life on earth. True life is not "the abundance of our possessions", but living in communion with and submission to the Lord who made us and who sent His Son to redeem us. Material provision and material possessions are part of that life, but they have to be kept in their place. Surrounded by a world that by and large does not really believe in God but in the ultimate reality of material things, we are called to show a different pattern and an integrated one. The way in which we deal with possessions is one part of the whole.

Perhaps the best illustration of this is in Leviticus 25, which speaks of Sabbatical years and the year of Jubilee. Every seventh year, the people of Israel were not to plant crops and not to harvest what grew, but to live on whatever came up by itself. The fiftieth year was to be kept in a similar way. That meant that in both the 49th and the 50th years there was no sowing and no real harvest, and it was three years between harvests. That is a long time. The obvious question was asked in v.20, "What will we eat in the seventh year if we do not plant or harvest our crops?" God's answer in v.21 was, "I will send you such blessing in the sixth year that the land will yield enough for three years." By this means Israel was called upon to demonstrate the truth summarized in Matthew 6:23, that if we seek first of all God's kingdom and His righteousness, all the things we need will be added to us. That took real trust. If God was real and trustworthy, they could do it, but supposing there was not enough to last those three years, and supposing the harvest in that 51st year was a failure? God was saying that as His people, living in a land specially given that they might demonstrate the right human way to live, they must learn to trust Him in material provision as well as in every other way, and to demonstrate this to the world.

I have outlined the way in which God has led members of the OMF to a particular stance on the question of material provision. There is, however, one other principle that governs everything. In some ways it relates to the first one, for it is concerned with God's faithfulness. The principle is that GOD'S WORK DONE IN GOD'S WAY WILL NEVER LACK GOD'S SUPPLY. We believe that. If God wants something done, is He going to withhold the very means that are necessary to do it? Would any human person command something to be done and not expect to have to supply the means? How much more the Lord of the universe. Therefore, we believe that if we are engaged in a work to which God has called us and for which He has commissioned us, we can legitimately expect Him to supply what is needed to get it done.

This has a valuable offshoot, for it means that if we are not doing the work God wants us to do and, equally important, if we are not doing it in the way He wants us to do it, He has a way of telling us. Lack of supply is a reason for us to ask questions. If we are embarking on something that is not God's will, then He can withhold the provision for it. If He wants to tell us that He approves, then He can move people to give. It is as simple as that.

These then are the principles on which the China Inland Mission and the Overseas Missionary Fellowship have worked for 120 years. They are not the only way in which to conduct Christian work, and they are not intended to be a superior way. But they are the way that God has called us to demonstrate His reality in a materialistic world. Sometimes people think we are crazy and imply that somewhere, hidden out of sight, there must be some answer other than God. Others in our over-stimulated environment would like to share in something simpler. At a recent missionary conference in Los Angeles, Dr Ralph Winter suggested that there is really no reason why any Christian work should lack supplies to carry on. Then he told us of some who, in their desire for a simpler lifestyle, have linked themselves with one or more missions or Christian organizations. They keep their secular jobs and go on earning their salaries, but instead of keeping their pay for themselves and giving what they can spare, they keep back only the equivalent of what the Christian worker in that organization is getting and hand the rest over to be used in God's work. If all the believing community acted in that way, we would have no problem determining what is a simple lifestyle, and Christian ministry would abound in funds. As someone has put it, "Faith giving must grow out of faith living."

The ultimate question is not what we do with our money but how deeply we trust in God, how much we believe that He exists and is the rewarder of those who diligently seek Him. Many say they believe, but do they trust? Abraham one day was told to take his son, his only son, whom he loved, and to go up a mountain that God would show him and there sacrifice his son. By this stage, Abraham had learned that God is utterly faithful and real. So next morning he was up early and off to the mountain. As Isaac accompanied his father up the steep incline, having left the rest of the company behind, he looked around for the sacrifice and could not see it. So Isaac said, "The fire and the wood are here, but where is the lamb for the burnt offering?" Abraham answered, "*God Himself will provide* the lamb for the burnt offering, my son." They went on to the altar and Abraham took the knife to kill his son. At that eleventh hour and 59th minute, God stepped in and told him not to do it. "Now I know that you fear God," He said. And as Abraham looked around, sure enough there in a thicket he saw a ram caught by its horns ready to be sacrificed. Coincidence? Abraham did not think so. He was doing God's work, and he believed God would provide as He had always done. So Abraham called that place *Jehovah Jireh* — the Lord will provide.

That motto *Jehovah Jireh* has been with the CIM/OMF from its beginning, for we believe it to be true. The Lord is the living God and He will provide for His people's needs. After all, our greatest need was for a Lamb to take away the sin of the world, and He provided that, and in doing so did not spare the life of His own only Son. If He provided that, will He not also with Him give us all things?

(DR JAMES H TAYLOR IS THE GENERAL DIRECTOR OF OMF AND THE GREAT-GRANDSON OF HUDSON TAYLOR, FOUNDER OF THE MISSION.)

1 This story and many others about Hudson Taylor can be found in *Biography of James Hudson Taylor*, published by OMF and Hodder & Stoughton.

Chapter One

OUR DAILY BREAD

The experiences of men and women who trusted God for their next meal.

"GIVE US THIS DAY ..."

When I was a student at the Lawas Bible School in Sarawak, Malaysia, the day came when I had no rice. My home village was three days' walk away in the interior of Sarawak, though only fifteen minutes by plane. I had no means of contacting my parents, but I prayed, "Father, I have no money and no rice. Will you please speak to my parents and cause them to send money and rice for me today?"

The next morning, about 10.30, I heard my name being called. Going to the window and looking out, I saw a boat driver whom I knew. Lawas Bible School is on the opposite side of the river from the town and the airport, and there is no bridge, so everything comes by boat.

"Quickly, quickly!" the boat driver called to me. "Take this tin of rice, it is sent to you by someone at the airline office."

When I looked at the tin and saw my name on it in my father's handwriting, I realized that God had answered my prayer already! Then I opened the tin and found inside an envelope containing M$50 (US$22).

(ALAU DE ROSS, EAST MALAYSIA)

"WHAT WILL WE EAT TOMORROW?"

Khru Jarern became full-time pastor of Khoksam-rong Church in Central Thailand at the end of November 1981. He was given no promise of full support by the church, although he did have some income from the renting of his fields and his house elsewhere. He lived in the church house on the church land.

One day Jarern was running out of food and had no money at all to buy rice for the family. That same day a member of the Chinese Church in Takhli, 65 km north of Khoksamrong, had been on a business trip to Lopburi, 35 km south of Khoksamrong. He boarded the bus at Lopburi and paid his full fare to return to Takhli, but felt very disturbed and restless. As the bus came into Khoksamrong he felt he had to get off and find out what the problem was. The Chinese Church in Takhli has very little contact with the majority of churches in Central Thailand, so he knew nothing at all about the church in Khoksamrong. However, he inquired whether there was a church in the town or around and, when he found there was, he went to one of the rice shops and ordered a sack of rice to be delivered to the pastor's house. So, as Jarern was praying about food and rice for his family, a sack of rice appeared over the horizon, completely unexpectedly.

On another occasion, Jarern's family ate the last of their food for the evening meal. When their ten-year-old son asked what they would eat tomorrow, the parents simply said, "We don't know. We will pray." So they prayed together and went to bed. During the night there was a heavy rainfall, and Jarern went out to close off the broken-down corner of the rice field. He felt something slippery under his feet and realized it was fish! He quickly called the rest of the family and they were able to collect enough fish to feed them for quite a while.

(STORY CONTRIBUTED BY THAILAND AREA DIRECTOR)

IMPOSSIBLE TO LIVE ON THAT!

As soon as I returned to Japan after my studies in Singapore, I had an interview with the OMF Home Council. We were not finally accepted, but my fiancee Izu and I were asked to go to Sapporo to work with OMFers there. We needed experience of church planting work, for until then we had only done student work. We were planning to get married that October.

Although we were asked to work in Sapporo, the Council did not help us financially. I did have a small amount of money for our wedding, but it would not be enough for our expenses for the next ten months. Then, one month before our planned wedding day, Izu's father died and I had to travel from Tokyo to Osaka to help the family. Of course our wedding had to be postponed, and so I went to Sapporo alone. I was thankful to God that a Christian friend gave me a half-price air ticket, which was even cheaper than the train fare.

Arriving in Sapporo, I went to see the pastor of my home church, Hokuei Church. He told me, "Although the Home Council decided you should help the congregation at Sakae Church, the members feel that they have been forced to accept you as an interim pastor, and they are unhappy about it. They have not prepared anything for you, and you have to find yourself a place to live." I thanked the Lord that I had come to Sapporo alone, for if Izu had been with me she would have felt very lonely in this area that was strange to her. I asked God's help to be humble enough to accept this hardship. Though the church did not welcome me, the Lord was with me, and there was peace and quietness deep in my heart. A kind Chinese lady from Hokuei

25

Church offered me a room for a while so that I could hunt for an apartment.

On my first Sunday there I went to the place where the Sakae congregation met for Sunday worship. Eight Japanese people were there with OMFer Rita Milligan. I sensed a strange and uneasy atmosphere, and sat in the back row. Rita introduced me to the congregation after the service and, as I anticipated, they did not show any sign of a warm welcome. However I smiled and introduced myself according to Japanese custom.

The church leaders decided that they would allow me to preach once a month and would support me by 1,000 yen per month (worth US$2.50 at that time). I still vividly remember Rita's perplexed face when she told me this. But God answered my prayers, and to my surprise I was calm with joy inside. I had no bad feeling or sense of insecurity. Later, Hokuei Church increased their support to 16,000 yen a month, but it was still impossible for me to live on such a small amount. The average monthly salary of college graduates at that time was 80,000 yen. However, I understood that this was a precious opportunity for me to learn OMF's financial policy, and I accepted this by faith without making any appeal to others.

A few weeks later, I found an old wooden apartment house for rent in the Sakae Church area. Immediately I prayed, "Lord, if this is the place for us to live in, give me a low rent." Then I phoned the owner, and he told me that the rent was 8,000 yen. This was cheap compared with other places. But he continued, "From your voice it seems to me that you are in your early fifties and reliable. Would you like to take the responsibility of caring for the apartment? If so I could let you rent it for half price." Half price, 4,000 yen per month! I thanked the Lord in

26

my heart. How wonderful that He even used my hoarse voice!

While living in that apartment after we were married, my wife and I had many opportunities to witness to the other residents, who were mostly manual labourers. One believed in Jesus and many others were interested in the gospel. A carpenter, who came to our room almost every day, offered us his brand new refrigerator when he knew that we did not have one. Pastor Saito also gave us a bicycle, so that we could save on travel expenses. We planted vegetables along the roadside and had a good crop, although I did not have proper agricultural knowledge. Sometimes unexpected visitors came and gave us generous gifts which met our daily needs.

When I look back to that period, I do not know how we managed to survive on such a small amount of money. However, *Jehovah Jireh* provided all things we needed in different ways, so often ways beyond our thought, when we prayed to Him.

(NAOYUKI MAKINO, FROM JAPAN, NOW WORKS IN THAILAND)

PASTOR'S EXAMPLE

The Lord was blessing one of the churches in Bangkok with weekly converts and with the knowledge that the Lord was working in their midst.

However, the church was not a wealthy one. Many members were quite poor, or were students, and although there were some professional people in the congregation, finances were quite tight for the many expenses. In particular, the church had a large programme for training and for evangelistic outreach, and such were the financial strictures that there was a real possibility that some of the programmes would have to be cut or curtailed.

One Sunday morning the pastor, a married man with two small pre-schoolers, told the church that he would no longer draw his salary. He lived on the church premises and so had a roof over his head. Members could provide in kind, for examples bananas from their gardens. He would trust the Lord to provide enough for himself and his family, believing that the Lord would not let His servant lack. Outreach with the gospel is very dear to the Lord's heart and the pastor felt confident that God would not fail them.

For more than six months he lived by faith in this way, believing and experiencing the Lord's provision for all his needs. At time there were hardships, however, and he was reduced to having to trap and eat sparrows.

The church finally felt that this situation was not right or glorifying to God, even though they were seeing much blessing. The members realized that they needed to give more and fully support their pastor, and at the same time a spontaneous love-offering was held one Sunday morning for him and his family. The gifts overflowed, and there was much joy in giving accompanied by an abundance of love in the Lord.

The church learned the priority of outreach and evangelism over personal comfort, through seeing this in their pastor's life. They learned that the Lord does supply, and that they themselves had a duty and a responsibility to support the Lord's servant. Perhaps we too in times of financial reductions and restrictions can learn some old lessons as well as new ones, and launch out in the work that really is close to God's heart.

(STORY CONTRIBUTED BY THAILAND AREA DIRECTOR)

CHICKENS STILL WARM!

How good our heavenly Father has been to us through this quarter when board money was reduced! Far from being short we have had ample, enabling us to share with others too. I hope others of the Fellowship have also found this. We have had gifts of rice and of eggs, and some lovely fruit on a few occasions. A couple of days ago a neighbour brought two chickens "because the children are home from Chefoo." They were still warm, but welcome nonetheless! The final touch was when an American naval base supermarket decided to unload some slow-moving foodstuffs, which were all quite edible and provided good protein for Cecil Moar who was staying with us after having had hepatitis.

(AUDREY PATTISSON, THEN IN KOREA)

SCRAPING THE BARREL

As of December 29, 1982, the Philippines Home Council had a balance of only ₱13.88 (less than US$1). Nothing could be given for our January allowance, not even food for one week. But just before the year ended, a personal gift to our family came which kept us through a week of drought. In reality it wasn't a drought because, when the Council was unable to give, the Lord provided through other means. Then by January 6 ₱31,490 ($2,250) had been received, more than enough for the needs of the Council, including us home staff members.

Sunday February 20, 1983 is a significant date for us because God once more proved Himself faithful in supplying for our daily needs. We had eaten our breakfast and there was no more rice to cook for lunch. We were again scraping the bottom of the barrel. We left home to go to the Sunday worship service and, just before we entered the sanctuary, a brother handed me an envelope. In it was an amount more than enough to buy a sack of rice. Praise the Lord! He is never late!

(WILLIAM LAYDA, AT THIS TIME EXECUTIVE SECRETARY OF THE PHILIPPINES HOME COUNCIL, NOW WORKS IN EAST MALAYSIA)

SHOPPING LIST

The following are the things the Lord provided through Japanese friends, Christian and non-Christian, during the month of January: 1 kg bacon, 1 cake, 1 lb onions, 1 small tin peaches, 1 packet peas, 2½ lbs pork meat for roasting, 1 litre milk, 1 sponge cake, 1 kg ham, 250 gm cheese, 1 packet biscuits, 1 large carrot, 300 gms mushrooms, 2 packets sweets, 6 oranges, 1 lb apples and a family meal out.

Sounds like a Christmas shopping list! Can anyone doubt that the Lord provides?

(PAUL & JANET PIKE, THEN IN JAPAN)

Chapter Two

THE LITTLE THINGS

God is concerned about the little things in life. Everything from a lost negative to buying a pair of shoes.

"My God shall supply ..."

Following the Manorom road accident in January 1978, when five missionaries and seven children were killed, those of us personally involved and all the team at Manorom hospital experienced the Lord's provision and caring love in many wonderful ways, large and small. Here is just one small example.

It was *so* hard to believe that our lively, bright little five-year-old Johnny was really gone from us for that long time till we would meet again in heaven. Suddenly photos became very precious. We had a number of nice black-and-white studies for which we were very thankful. There was, however, one particular colour print that a friend had taken a few months before the accident. This portrayed Johnny's happy liveliness just as he was. How we would have loved an enlargement! We had in fact been given the negative, but Rosemary was almost certain that, in a burst of enthusiastic spring cleaning, she had thrown it away. How sorry she was! I hunted high and low in the vain hope of finding it, but to no avail.

Some months later our housegirl asked Rosemary about the cost of colour photos, and Rosemary replied that if you had to buy the film it was quite costly. "No," said L. "I have the negative already." Then it came to light that, all those months before, the dear girl had kept the negative out of the rubbish and had stored it safely in an envelope at home.

How full our hearts were as we realized the great goodness of our dear Lord, in so ordering events for our joy and comfort.

Our lovely lively picture of Johnny on our bedroom

wall is precious to us. People seeing it have said, "It really makes you smile straight back at him, it's so real." Johnny's sister, who has never met him but is *very* like him, can't wait to see him in heaven either, and the photo has meant a lot to her, as well as to all of us.

"My God *shall* supply all your need according to His riches in glory by Christ Jesus."

(PETER & ROSEMARY FARRINGTON)

SPECIAL TREATS

It promised to be rather a lean three months. The housekeeping allowance for each household had suffered a ten percent cut, a very rare occurrence. Of course, there would be no real problem. None of us would be anywhere near starvation, or even losing weight. It would simply mean that there would be no occasional special treats for the next quarter.

But God, like any loving father, *likes* to give his children special treats sometimes. "If you then, being evil, know how to give good gifts to your children ..." well, so does God, only much more so!

The OMF Mission Home hostess in Kuala Lumpur received a telephone call from one of the stores in town. "We have a batch of damaged tins here. Would you be interested in them at a fraction of the normal cost? You would — good! Will you send someone down to collect them?"

This happened from time to time, but as there was never any guarantee what the tins would contain, we wondered what was going to be in this batch. When the tins arrived at the Mission Home there was great rejoicing and amazement. They all contained expensive

American pie fillings — cherry, blueberry, peach, apple. These were normally beyond our *regular* budget, but this "thin" quarter God chose to give them to us at a price that even we could afford. We all had plenty of special treats those three months.

(GILLIAN HUNT, THEN WORKING IN MALAYSIA)

EXPERIENCE WHAT YOU TEACH

A number of years ago I had holidays in March, and on my way back to Manorom Christian Hospital I stopped in Bangkok. As it was often difficult to buy stamps and airforms up country, I drew out the remainder of my remittance and stocked up. Then I discovered that because of shortage of funds there would be no personal remittance at all for the next quarter! I had my fare back to Manorom and that was all.

The first month passed without any difficulty. I could write home, I had soap and toothpaste, and I didn't need any cash. I was short of a uniform for duties, but then a parcel arrived from a fellow missionary in the Philippines. She had a uniform which she wasn't using. Would it be of any use to me? A little alteration and I could wear it.

As time passed I began to feel the crunch — my supplies of stamps and airforms were running out, and I needed other things too. Just at that time an anonymous donor in the United States sent $20 to be given to the neediest missionary on the field, and it was decided I should have it! Praise the Lord that this was sufficient until the end of the quarter, and for the new quarter there was a substantial allowance.

More recently there were several periods when the personal allowance did not seem to stretch out the whole three months. I was at Nongbua Hospital then, and we were having problems with some of the nurse aides. Many of them had come straight from school; most were not used to handling money and had no idea how to live within their income. They thought in typical oriental fashion that everything could be bought "on tick" and paid for at the end of the month. Often the amount owing was more than their wages, so money was borrowed at interest. One girl ran away because the interest owing on the money she had borrowed was more than her monthly wages! I tried to advise and urge the girls to live within their income, and not to buy without paying cash. I felt it was because I had to teach this to the girls that the Lord wanted me to experience it too.

One quarter there were two events which I knew would take some extra money. The first was holidays. I was booked to go to Huahin, and so in faith I set off. As it turned out, my travelling expenses were cut to a minimum. The weekend before I left we had a youth conference with a visiting Thai speaker from Bangkok, who had driven up in his own car with his wife and small baby. They gladly offered me a ride through to Bangkok, and all it cost me was 1.50 baht for a bus fare from the suburbs into the Mission Home! For the second part of the journey to Huahin I went third class on the train at half price with my "clergy" pass, given to all religious workers! On the return trip I had a lift in the Superintendent's car. He would accept only a small contribution towards the petrol, and then I had just a short train trip and the bus to Nongbua to pay for.

The second event, which followed a couple of weeks

later, was the annual graduation service of nurse aides. As I was to take part in the service I needed a long-sleeved uniform, but the only one I had was badly ink-stained on the skirt. What to do? There was no money to buy material so I looked at it and decided that by cutting up an old short-sleeved uniform I would have enough material to replace the complete side panel of the skirt. Often clothes that I have altered don't look very nice, especially as I do it infrequently, but the Lord undertook that time. I undid the panel, cut another out of the back of the old uniform and sewed it in without any problem, and it looked so good afterwards! I wore it at the graduation and no one realized that it was a repair job!

That quarter the Lord also gave me a bonus. We had a visit from a former nurse aide, an older Christian girl, and she gave me a lovely green maxi dress. That style was in vogue then, and I had frequently looked at them in shops and turned away with a sigh! But the Lord gave me one — my favourite colour, a good fit, no alterations needed and the style I liked! I still have it, although it is getting rather worn now.

Since I started writing this the Lord has provided again! In June when on holiday I lost a 100 baht note and, in spite of every care, my account went into the red. The next quarter's remittance came in early so I was able to square everything up. I divided what was left into three parts and decided how much I would use each month, but in spite of much care I overspent for July. Then just yesterday a $10 personal gift came in — enough to see me through August without touching what I had allocated for September.

Recently I have been reading *God's Smuggler* in which Brother Andrew relates one of his experiences in living by faith. Both he and his wife were very careful in spending money, as the less they used the more they had for the work. The clothes they wore came from a pile of used clothing which had been given them for refugee work. One day they were going out to dinner and his wife said, "I have nothing to wear." When he looked over her wardrobe it was true. There were dresses for everyday wear but nothing for a special occasion. He writes, "Suddenly I saw that this was part of a whole pattern of poverty into which we had fallen, a dark brooding pinched attitude that hardly went with the Christ of the open heart that we were preaching to others." So his wife bought a new dress, and when the third child arrived they went out and bought him some new clothes.

I realized that I was falling into this dark brooding attitude, and reading this has jerked me out of it.

(MARGARET OGILVIE HAS WORKED IN THAILAND FOR OVER THIRTY YEARS)

WEALTH ... WITH NO
ADDED TROUBLE

OMF financial provision is through the pooled gifts of interested supporters, and the salary for office workers like us comes from the same source.

For the first four months of 1984 income in our country was only 80 percent of our prayer goal, and in order to share in this shortfall the Executive Secretary and I agreed together to take only 80 percent of our salaries — joyfully and thankfully!

With one heart we prayed to the Lord for our daily bread, confident that He would supply according to our need. Before the end of the next month, May, He had provided fully for the support of our missionaries and for our salaries.

The Lord did not ignore my personal needs either. At that time, meditating on 2 Chronicles, I thought about the command, "Walk before me in righteousness." I realized that he who had received full forgiveness should give himself unconditionally to the Lord. At that time the Lord brought to my attention the financial difficulties of the church I was attending and impressed on me my responsibility about this.

Having committed myself totally to the Holy Spirit I realized that I could trust my heavenly Father for all my material needs, knowing that He would provide. And I discovered how accurately the Lord keeps His accounts. When I received my salary for June I set aside the money I would need for food, travel and tithes. The amount left was about US$90. At that moment I was overawed to think that I had so much money over and in humility handed it back to the Lord, saying, "Lord, this is too much, I can't look after this. Please look after it for me. When I need something I will let you know."

The next day, through a sister, the Lord sent me some pairs of stockings that I needed. He also saw my mouth watering in front of a fruit stall that day and later, by the hand of a visitor to our office, sent us a water melon. As well as this, just when I needed it, He sent on one occasion ten dollars and on another five dollars. In addition to this He gave me the joy and peace of trusting Him fully.

However, perhaps to deflate my pride, He then showed me that He is never our debtor. Before the end of July, through the goodness of our supporters, the Lord had sent us considerably more than our prayer goal. Our Chairman was aware of the need of our Executive Secretary and his family, who had twice foregone his bonus salary, and instructed us to apply the surplus to that need.

At the same time, along with my July salary I received a bonus of $100. I don't know if this was the Lord's calculation of interest on what I had given back to Him, but I do know that, in addition, He has heaped on me blessings from heaven beyond counting and I want to thank my heavenly Father for His visiting me and for the experience of His touch.

With my life bound to the Holy Spirit, I have learned to be content in whatever state I am.

"The blessing of the Lord brings wealth,

And He adds no trouble to it" (Proverbs 10.22)

(TESTIMONY FROM A MEMBER OF STAFF IN AN ASIAN HOME COUNCIL OFFICE).

SHOES

I needed good walking shoes for autumn but had little money, so I prayed about the right use of it before meeting Catherine Ranger for shopping. A friend of hers, hearing of me but not knowing my need, gave her US$60 for me! This paid for my shoes and also for other things I needed.

(DAPHNE ROBERTS, THEN WORKING IN KOREA)

MIND THE KEYS!

The young lady who is our cashier here at Manorom Christian Hospital in Thailand is aptly named "Bunch of Gold". One evening some years ago, while she was still a relatively new Christian and also a new motor bike rider, she had a serious accident on her way home. She lives about two kilometres up the river from Manorom market and as she turned right on approaching her home she failed to notice a motor bike coming fast in the opposite direction.

She was hit hard and received quite serious facial injuries and a broken wrist. The impact caused her handbag, which was in the basket on the front of the motor bike, to be catapulted into the river. In the urgency of the situation the bag was unnoticed. It did not sink but floated down river in the direction of the market. Later it was seen and fished out of the water by someone who, miraculously, was constrained to return it to her home with the contents intact.

There was even more significance attached to this event in that the young lady had accidentally taken home an extremely important set of keys from the hospital *in that handbag*!

Wonderfully, she made a complete recovery from her badly broken jaw, and testified to how she had proved the Lord through that painful experience. She is now a leader in Manorom Church. As for the keys, they are now always faithfully handed in after use and kept safely at the hospital.

(STORY FROM A MISSIONARY WORKING AT MANOROM CHRISTIAN HOSPITAL)

Chapter Three

AND THE BIG

An unexpected bill, a tax payment and a mountain of debt provide God with an opportunity to show His faithfulness.

OUR MOUNTAIN-MOVING GOD

Little did I realize on June 21, 1980, as I confidently declared "I do," that I was beginning the most important stretch of my missionary training. As Mike and I joined in marriage, our financial debts were joined too! These totaled US$14,000 and included a car payment, university loans and a bowling loan from Mike's professional bowling days on the US pro-bowling tour. It was our conviction that we should never again go into debt. If God was guiding us into an area requiring finance that we did not have, then we would look to Him to supply.

Since our goal for our ministry in marriage was to serve the Lord in a cross-cultural capacity overseas, it was necessary to liquidate our debts before going. We both worked to help increase our rate of payment and figured it would take three to four years to pay off our debt completely.

It was a brisk April day during our first year of marriage when God began preparing the way for His faithfulness to be manifested in our lives as never before. It was a good day for a walk and a talk. Mike had something on his heart and he wanted to break it to me gently.

"Sue, the Lord has laid a concern on my heart that I want to share with you." There was a long pause and then Mike continued, "But before I do, I want to be sure you understand that what I'm about to say is not a negative reflection on you in any way."

"Okay," I replied, wondering what was to follow.

"Sue, these past nine months have been really great, but I feel that something is missing from my relationship with the Lord. I sense that in wanting to be a good

45

husband, I've not been trusting the Lord as fully as I did before we were married. I was wondering if we might commit ourselves anew to trusting God more fully in every area of our life together." We sealed our commitment in prayer that day and began looking for opportunities to trust Him more fully.

Opportunities came. In August, while we were attending a missions conference, the Lord confirmed in our hearts His leading to a cross-cultural ministry overseas. Now all that was needed was some seminary study for Mike and our debts to be paid in full — two goals that seemed insurmountable, considering that Mike was already nudging the thirty age bracket. But God was working. He began instilling within Mike, who had been quite resistant to the thought of further academic training, a keen desire to go to seminary — a desire thwarted only by our "mountain" of debts.

It was Friday evening, October 17, 1981. Sue was in the living room and I was in my study reading Arthur Mathews' *Born for Battle.* I became so intrigued with the Mark 11 passage of Scripture Mathews refers to, that I began studying the passage for myself. I discovered that Jesus uses the word "faith" differently from the New Testament writers. When Jesus uses "faith" it is an exceptionally strong word meaning one's trust in God is so powerful that it transforms the physical surroundings.

Jesus wanted to teach his disciples the conditions for having this kind of faith. Firstly, *we cannot doubt.* Jesus says, "Have faith in God ... If anyone says to this mountain, 'Go throw yourself into the sea,' and does not doubt in his heart ... " Next Jesus teaches that *we must have an attitude of expectation* that God will do it, "...

but believes that what he says will happen, it will be done for him." Lastly, *the believer must be clean before God and man,* "If you hold anything against anyone, forgive him, so that your Father in heaven may forgive you your sins."

As Jesus taught this vivid object-lesson, He and His disciples were traveling from Bethany into Jerusalem, and Jesus very likely pointed to the Mount of Olives for visual impact as they passed by it.

We didn't have a physical mountain hindering us; we had a "financial" mountain, with an altitude at that point in our marriage of $10,000! As I finished studying the Mark 11 passage I drew a mountain on a card, wrote our current debt-figure at the top of the mountain and dated it. At the bottom of the mountain I wrote Jesus' words, "Have faith in God."

Then I got on my knees and prayed: "Father, You have put within my heart a strong desire to go to seminary. I do not understand your timing, as you know fully about our financial obligations. I do not want to presume that you will take care of this debt in a supernatural way. You have given us employment enabling us to make monthly payments, for which we give you thanks. At the same time, Lord, we believe you are clearly guiding us to go overseas and I'm not getting any younger. At the rate we're going it'll take another couple of years to pay off our debts and then a year or two to go to seminary. But Lord, based on your Word, I want to acknowledge to you my belief that you can and will take care of this financial mountain, whether it be through our continual monthly payments or in a supernatural way. Father, I believe you are fully able to work and by faith I expect you to work. I don't know how and I don't know when. I want to be clean before you so that you may work and do your good and perfect will in our lives."

As I finished praying I believed that I saw the word "Canceled" across the mountain I had drawn. I was sure of it! I was sure God had met with me, and was in fact leading me to seminary soon.

That same evening Mike shared with me "his" mountain passage and his assurance that the Lord was leading him back to school. I struggled for two days to believe with Mike's confidence that our God was able and willing to remove a debt He did not owe! By Sunday afternoon the Lord had so dealt with me that I joined Mike in believing that God was more than able to work. Together we began expecting the Lord to work basing our expectations on "our" mountain passage.

Able indeed! A week and one day later on Monday October 27, God began to work.

While I was at my job in our local church on Monday an elderly church member came to see me.

"Mike, I understand you want to go to seminary. Why don't you go?"

"Well," I said, "Sue and I have some financial obligations we need to take care of first."

"Mike, this past week the Lord has given me some extra money. All week long your name has been on my heart. I believe the Lord would have me give you some money. May I give you a check for $2,000?"

As quickly as a check can change hands, God chopped off the top fifth of our mountain! I was delighted and full of gratitude, but not surprised. I was expecting God to work and I saw this as God working through an individual who knew nothing of our debts, but was being moved by the Spirit of God. I shared with this friend our mountain passage and how God was using him to remove part of that mountain, though I did not tell him the total figure. I phoned Sue and she was ecstatic! We were convinced that God was clearly leading me back to seminary.

Two days later as I arrived at work, the elderly friend was waiting for me in the church parking lot.

"Mike, God has continued to lay your name on my heart and I believe He wants me to help remove some more of that mountain for you," he said handing me a folded check.

I went into my office and prayed, "Lord, I don't know the amount of this check, but I thank you for proving your faithfulness in our lives." I opened the check and thought I saw an amount of $300, but actually it was a check for $3,000! In two days God had physically removed one-half of our mountain! By then I could confidently declare, "I know that God is saying, 'Go!'"

I made application to the Trinity Evangelical Divinity School and was accepted to begin my course work in January, 1982. The $5,000 the Lord had supplied was applied specifically to two of our debts, not to the $1,200 I would need for my first quarter's tuition and books. We could only believe that God would continue to prove Himself faithful. It was now the end of October. Little did we suspect how God would prove His faithfulness in the next two months before my first quarter began.

We were traveling home from a previewing of the Hudson Taylor film when the idea of cutting back on our living expenses popped into my mind and nearly as quickly popped out of my mouth. Mike and I were soon embarking on an adventure that would prepare us well for a missionary lifestyle as well as continue to prove God's faithfulness.

At that time we had two cars and a fairly large apartment, nothing extravagant, but more than was needed for a seminary student and his wife who were potential missionaries. We advertized one of our cars for sale and inquired into a possibility of housesitting at a low rent from January 1, three days before Mike would begin seminary. We received permission from our landlord to sublet our apartment for two months until our lease expired in February, so that we would be free to begin housesitting. All we had to do was find someone!

In the meantime, we received news that I would be losing my job. I worked for the city in a seemingly "secure" job, but the city had gone into debt and now had to release 100 employees including me. My last day of work was the same as Mike's — December 24, 1981.

What timing! We found ourselves thrown completely on God. Now we were both facing unemployment, and no one wanted to rent our apartment, which meant that we might have to pay double rent. We had nothing to cover expenses for seminary, and yet we believed, with a sure knowledge of His will, that Mike was to begin seminary on January 4.

God again proved Himself faithful. By December 31 He provided someone to rent our apartment, someone else to purchase one of our cars, and an unexpected gift of $500. With great rejoicing we moved into our new home on New Year's Day. Money from our returned escrow, the sale of the car, and the financial gift, provided Mike with just enough to pay for first quarter tuition and books three days later. Three weeks after that the Lord provided a full-time job for me, enabling us to live off my income and save for upcoming school bills.

We still had $5,000 to contend with on our "mountain", but this was in the form of long-term state loans that totaled a $70 montly payment. With God's provision of my job we could afford to maintain these payments, at least for the time being.

In October of 1982, Ben Draper, the OMF Candidate Secretary for USA, talked to me about the possibility of Sue attending school with me to do some refresher course work. The thought of going to school together seemed like a dream, but at first we didn't take his suggestion seriously. After all, Sue was working so that I could attend school. Who would pay the bills if she was sitting in classes?

The Lord moved us to pray about the possibility. We prayed, checked into the courses Sue could take, and considered the implications of quitting her job. Certainly we were willing to trust God, but was this the right thing to do? Our home city was hit very hard by the recession and many family men in our local church were unemployed. What type of testimony would it give if Sue quit a good job at this time? We sought counsel from our senior pastor and he felt Sue should attend seminary for at least one quarter, though he was also concerned about the local church situation.

At no other time in our lives had we felt so neutral about a decision. God would have to show us more definitely His will in this matter. Not being able to make a decision, we wrote to the leaders of OMF informing them of the various factors in the situation, and asking them if it was imperative that Sue attend seminary. We sent that letter on a Monday.

On the following Friday, before OMF could reply, we received news that Sue was the recipient of an inheritance. The amount was sufficient to remove the remainder of our "financial mountain", to pay for my remaining school bills, as well as to allow Sue to resign from her job and go to school with me. And there was enough left over for us to live off until we would attend the OMF Candidate School in June, 1983. Again God was proving His faithfulness!

When I had seen the word "Canceled" across my mountain, God had in fact thrown it into the sea! The elements of true faith were there: not doubting that God was able, expecting Him to do His work in His way in accordance with His perfect will, and making sure that we were clean before Him and one another. The joy of experiencing God's faithfulness was ours in full. We hope this is only the beginning of a lifetime of taking God at His Word and proving Him totally faithful.

> "There is a living God;
> He has spoken in the Bible.
> He means what He says,
> And will do all that He has promised."
> — J. Hudson Taylor.

(MIKE & SUE ALFIERI NOW WORK IN JAPAN.)

"HE OPENETH HIS HAND ON HIGH"

The German school in Singapore, which some of our OMF children attend, had been planning to build new premises for some time.

In March 1982 we heard that each child attending the school would have to pay a S$10,000 debenture towards the cost of the new building. The payment would be due as soon as the agreement had been signed.

This news came as a terrible shock to us, for it meant that OMF would have to pay S$70,000 (US$33,000)! As we shared this with the children in the hostel, we were reminded that our God is the God of the impossible, and we encouraged them all to pray that the needed amount of money would come in time.

A few months later our Home Director in Germany wrote to tell us of different gifts coming in for this purpose. But there still seemed such a long way to go. Would we ever reach the $70,000? We kept on praying, and trusted that the Lord who had led us to this school would also provide for our needs.

In November we heard from the school that a final decision had been made about the land for the new school, and thought this meant we would have to pay immediately. We contacted OMF Headquarters and were told that the amount was almost complete — only $1,500 more was needed! If God had given so much already it would not be a problem for Him to send the rest; so we went on praying.

Two months later the school wrote and asked us to pay the money in two weeks time. "I wonder how much is still needed?" was my first thought. What a joy it was to hear that all $70,000 was in hand, and could be paid the next day! What a wonderful God we have. I was reminded of the song we used to sing at table in Chefoo School in the Philippines:

"Jehovah Jireh is His Name and He provides,
The Lord who died my soul to save, He will
provide.

53

He openeth His hand on high, every creature to
satisfy,
I'll trust Him as the days go by, for He provides."

(JOACHIM AND ANNEMARIE WESNER ARE THE HOSTEL PARENTS FOR OMF'S
SWISS AND GERMAN CHILDREN ATTENDING SCHOOLS IN SINGAPORE.)

WHERE WILL THE MONEY COME FROM?

"It is all very well to decide to put up some new buildings, but where will the money come from?" The British Isles Council at its 1983 annual meeting had just decided to build some sheltered housing on the estate of the retired workers' home in Pembury. Cornford House has spacious grounds and there was ample room for the addition of some single storey accommodation, which was clearly needed. God, however, had already begun to work.

Two retired couples had enjoyed for many years a house donated to the Mission for this very purpose in Sheringham, Norfolk. But following the death of his wife one man, finding the upstairs flat too inconvenient with his artificial leg, decided to leave to be nearer to his daughter. This prompted the other couple to think that they too should move south to be nearer their family. At just about the same time, a former CIM missionary left her house to the Mission. It was situated in Eastbourne on the south coast and was conveniently divided into two flats, one for the time being occupied but the other free. This provided just the opportunity needed to vacate the Sheringham house and put it on the market. After part of the proceeds had been used to put the Eastbourne house in prime condition, a small sum was left for the new development at Cornford House.

At the Ministers' Fraternal Christmas lunch, I found myself sitting next to a good friend who was also one of the trustees of a well-known Trust providing accommodation for Christian workers. I was interested to learn that the Trust house had been sold, as it was no longer meeting the need for which it had been set up, and heard some of the plans for the disbursement of the considerable sum of money now available. Since the object of the Trust was to provide housing for retired missionaries, the temptation to mention the Cornford House Development Project was almost too great. However, I respected our non-solicitation policy and kept quiet.

Upon returning to the office, I mentioned the incident to one of my colleagues, who added to the temptation by telling me that one of the other trustees was a former treasurer of the Mission.

"Do you think we ought to have a word with him?"

My colleague was prayerfully reticent, and no contact was made.

Some days later, however, a telephone call came from that former treasurer, enquiring whether there was some special need of funds for retired workers! So the opportunity to introduce the Cornford House Development Scheme arose. Imagine our delight when, several weeks later, another telephone call brought the information that no less than £80,000 had been earmarked as a gift towards our new sheltered housing scheme! What wonderful confirmation of the decision made nearly a year previously. There is no doubt at all that the Lord wants that particular building project to go ahead!

(JOHN WALLIS, OMF HOME DIRECTOR, UK)

THE FIRST FISH'S MOUTH

After I had written the last Quarterly Financial Report in January, I felt some unease at having mentioned the matter of the heavy demands expected in connection with Value Added Tax payments, because this could be taken as an "announcement of needs". Subsequently I received two letters confirming that some readers were unhappy about this.

Much as I needed those kindly criticisms, the Lord had dealt His own clear rebuke before either of those letters arrived. You will remember that I drew attention to the wonderful provision Jesus made while He was here on earth to meet a local tax requirement, through a coin in the mouth of the first fish that Peter drew out of the water. As we came to the end of January it was clear that we were faced with an enormous bill of over £20,000 to meet these back VAT payments. Hudson Taylor established a principle which we have always sought to follow, that accounts should be paid on presentation and debts should not be allowed to occur. The Financial Secretary accordingly agreed to make the VAT payment a priority in February, and we made the customary maximum allocation of funds to Singapore at the end of January, without holding anything back for the VAT payment.

The first batch of mail I opened in February included a legacy of over £23,000! To me, the Lord was saying once again, "You don't need to announce your needs to anybody. I am the Lord who sees and the Lord who will provide". Once again, His unbelieving disciple was rebuked as he opened "the first fish's mouth"!

(FROM A LETTER TO OMF PRAYER MEETINGS IN UK.)

FOR WHAT PURPOSES?

A Scottish lady who died in 1947 left the residue of her estate to the China Inland Mission. A number of payments were made in the early days, but the trustees did not accept the change of name from CIM to OMF in spite of its official recognition by the Charity Commission in London. So, after years of patient endeavour by our lawyers, the matter finally went before a court in Edinburgh. The judge, whose ruling ran to eleven pages, wholly supported OMF's claim to be the successor to CIM and thus cleared the way for all the residue capital and income to come to us, 32 years after the generous donor's death! When the total amount arrived it came to £90,000.

When the Lord sends us exceptionally large gifts such as this, a very heavy responsibility rests upon those who have to determine the correct use of the funds. Does the Lord see that we are going to have some very special needs in the near future, either in the expansion of the work in East Asia or perhaps to meet some extraordinary crisis? Those who went through the turbulent financial days of the withdrawal from China will recall how the Lord supplied all of our extraordinary needs in those days, very often in remarkable ways, and one can only echo that He is "just the same today."

(FROM A LETTER TO OMF PRAYER MEETINGS IN UK)

AN OPEN DOOR

No one had ever produced video-cassettes for Christian service in Asia before, at least not outside Japan, and certainly not with the scripting and production entirely in Asian hands. Many of our experienced professional friends counselled us against getting embroiled in such a new medium.

57

However, in Hong Kong the doorway was wide open. Every school was government-equipped to show videos, and 60 percent of the schools were in church hands. We had very little money, no property, no influential friends, and no precedents. But our Chairman, a fine Chinese Christian businessman, knew we must make a start somewhere.

Prayerfully we dug deep into our slender capital to buy the minimum equipment needed to make the most basic Christian videos, giving the importer the order with some trepidation. God seemed to confirm the move by sending us a £1000 gift the next day. Then the importer phoned to say that since some of the gear would have to be brought specially from Japan, we must pay a deposit — of almost triple the amount of this recent gift. We paid, and the next day a further gift of £2000 arrived.

Thus far, material provision was adequate, but what about space and personnel? Hong Kong's notoriously high rents gave us little hope of obtaining a place we could afford, and the goods were to be delivered to us very soon. Then we were offered, temporarily, a room in a parsonage that was scheduled for reconstruction, but on which the plans had run into a year or so's delay. The creative personnel — always the scarcest element in Christian communications — came when a Chinese group with much training and experience in other performing arts media unexpectedly invited us into a joint venture.

We started with a seminar, moved up to scripting, and now Hong Kong has a pool of vigorous, trained, mostly young Christian communicators to face the Christian future in this medium.

(DAVID HUNTLEY, ON LOAN TO FEBA.)

THRILLS FROM HOMESIDE OFFICES

March brought another of those extremely humbling experiences when one donor came to discuss with me how we might use £50,000! After consultation with OMF International Headquarters in Singapore we agreed that £20,000 would go to General Fund and £30,000 towards a number of very strategic projects overseas.

This donation was entered in our books just two days after the annual meeting of the Council for the British Isles, where it had been a privilege to explain once again for the benefit of some of our newer Council members the grounds for our confidence in the utter reliability of "laying the needs of the work before God in prayer". I would challenge anyone to sit at my desk for a month and still think otherwise.

For several years, sometimes twice a year, just when funds were very low, we have received substantial gifts, ranging from $10,000 to $30,000, from a gentleman in the midwest of the United States. We knew very little about him until we specifically inquired about four years ago. He was at that time in the printing business, and had a large, grown-up family of seven or eight children, all but one of whom were in the Lord's service. It was a thrill to learn of this dedicated Christian family. I believe the son has now taken over the business but we still receive large gifts, the most recent being for $25,000.

One Thursday morning during office prayers in the USA we were praying specially for the Lord's financial provision. All was rather "low" and "dark" that morning.

During prayer time the morning mail arrived, and after I returned to my desk my secretary, with some alacrity and a smile, handed me an envelope containing a check for $50,000. Five minutes later I looked into the main office, and there came Home Director Dan Bacon waving another check for $50,000 — from the same donor, but really from the Lord! It made our day and went to fill up the coffers in the field! Yes, we gathered and thanked our heavenly Father.

Chapter Four

SOMETHING OLD, SOMETHING NEW, SOMETHING BORROWED ...

A battered shaving brush, a second-hand tooth, and ten rolls of wallpaper bought in a sale all prove to be God's provision for His children.

A BATTERED SHAVING BRUSH

Both my wife and I were born with the proverbial silver spoon in our mouths, having all the supposed advantages of upper middle class suburbia at our disposal. Upon our arrival in Thailand we found that this spoon, along with our American values, had turned to aluminum. We were faced with a culture in which promptness, privacy, convenience and hygiene were not highly esteemed. Yet we discovered that one can live and even thrive on simple things in the realms of food, transportation, clothing and housing. A careful examination of the Bible has confirmed to me that a simple lifestyle, suitable to the culture one is in, is not only the most practical but also the most biblical in light of the needs of the poor and of evangelism among them today.

Like so many young people I had been isolated from the relatively poor in my home community in USA. The poor were those who lived on "the other side of the tracks", an area we scrupulously avoided. Yet now we found that hardly a day went by without a beggar passing our doorstep. The Thai church also forced us to see the needs of the poor. One third of our church members had leprosy, another third were illiterate, and the majority lived on a mere subsistence level, what the Thai call "seek in the morning and eat at night." Thailand, however, is better off than many countries, since in today's world some 800 million people are destitute and 10,000 die of starvation daily. No longer could we remain "National Geographic" Christians whose only exposure to the poor is through glossy photos in magazines. God made us more aware of how to steward our money as well as what level of subsistance we should live at.

The Thai have taught me the greatest lessons in the school of contentment. "Mr Itch" is a leprosy patient who got his name because of his habit of scratching his leprous skin. He is fairly well off for a man with leprosy. He owns his land debt-free, and along with his wife is even able to save a little. Yet the number of shirts he owns can be counted on one hand, he has a $5 watch which he is unable to set, he has no transportation, only fourth grade education, and no electricity or modern conveniences. Some may say that he just doesn't know how badly off he really is. But the fact remains that he is content. His contentment is not based on anything which the west labels essential, but it is biblical, deeply rooted in his relationship with Jesus Christ rather than in society's whims.

A symbol of what I've learned about the simple life style is my bruised and battered shaving brush. I was almost thirty before I learned to use one! A can of shaving cream costs over $5 in Thailand, and in search of an alternative I made the amazing discovery that shaving cream is merely soap! By using a brush I figure I've saved about $150 over a four-year period.

Another symbol is our 25-year-old bicycle. In the States I felt my two cars were a necessity. But now I've discovered that riding a bike or using public transport opens up many opportunities to minister to people. My language supervisor said her best times to witness have come on crowded Thai buses. Another missionary refused to buy a motorbike, preferring a bicycle because "this way the Thai Christians will have no excuses about not witnessing. We can all go together on our bikes to do visitation. No one needs to rely on the missionary's vehicle."

(LARRY & PAULA DINKINS WORK IN THAILAND)

CHEAP WALLPAPER

When Ron and I moved to Bristol to live in OMF's Regional Centre there, we inherited a worn and unattractive stair carpet and a hall that had not been decorated for twenty years. We put up with it for a while, but after four years of heavy wear, the carpet showed ample evidence that it had had its day. It would have to be replaced, and for this we would need about forty yards of carpet which would cost about £400, not including underlay. Of course I would have liked a fitted carpet, but that seemed out of the question for a Regional Centre.

Some months after this, the old children's hostel at Maxwell House was sold and we were offered its sixty yards of pale-grey Wilton stair carpet, with underlay. So here was the new carpet! However, we knew it would be foolish to lay it without doing some decorating. The house is a large three-storey one and the estimate for getting the hall and stairs decorated was over £600. In addition there had been serious flooding in the basement and this would cost anything from £150 to £1,500 to put right. It all seemed impossible.

At this point we went to the OMF Council meetings and were able to share our problem with Guy Longley of the Central Office staff. As he returned to Sevenoaks he was mulling it over in his mind and wondering what the answer could be. We were all praying about it, and when I saw some cheap wallpaper a day or two later I decided to go ahead and buy it in the faith that we could do something ourselves. It was impossible to know how much we would need for a hall with so many staircases and small walls, but we bought the only ten rolls the shop had.

Back at his desk, Guy opened a letter from a cousin

of mine who had recently been left some money. The letter read, "For Ron and Kathy Preece to use for something for their house which they could not otherwise have," and enclosed was a gift of £250. It was followed by another gift of £100 with similar instructions. Telling us about it, Guy commented, "I cannot but think that the Lord has prompted this gift to meet this need at this time."

With such an encouragement to go ahead, I appealed on local radio for a retired person who wanted to earn some money, and together we began the mammoth task. It involved painting 17 doors and two ceilings, and covering the walls with emulsion and paper. We used *all* that cheap paper! We now have a fully fitted Wilton carpet right to the top of the house. All this was done for about £150, so there was enough money left to have new curtains in the lounge, as well as to meet half the cost of having that room professionally decorated. The Lord truly does provide more abundantly than we could ask or think.

(KATHY PREECE, UK HOME STAFF)

TEETH ...

When we were working in Singapore my wife and I used to visit a Christian lady dentist there who always treated us very generously. On one occasion I had to have a gold crown put on one of my teeth, and she was most apologetic, saying, "This is going to be rather expensive, because I do have to charge you for the gold."

When I went back to have the crown fitted, however, the dentist told me with great delight that a Chinese lady patient had had a gold tooth extracted and had not wanted anything for it. The dentist had immediately thought of me, and was able to use the gold from this other tooth to make the crown for mine.

(ALLAN KNIGHT)

A suitable footnote to the above comes from the OMF UK office:

A dentist sent us £40 from a grateful patient. It was a refund from some old gold dentures, so we were advised, "Don't throw away your old teeth."

The occasional stone in the rice always seems to connect with my not-so-strong teeth, and so I had to go to the dentist in Korea. He informed me that the amount of work necessary would cost $200. I didn't have anywhere near that amount of money in my personal account, and so thought and prayed for a minute. As I prayed it seemed to me that from a health point of view I really should go ahead with this work. As it would take a couple of months the dentist was happy for the amount to be paid off in instalments.

However, this was not necessary. When I arrived home after this initial visit, there was a letter informing me that two months previously a friend in Australia had given $200 as a personal gift, and this amount had now been credited to my account. How great and loving is our God who answers even before we call!

(CECILY MOAR)

SUMMER BLESSINGS

We usually reckon our receipts in pounds and pence, but they do not reveal the whole story of the Lord's goodness. I don't need to tell you how expensive holidays are nowadays, but here too the Lord knows the weakness of our mortal frames and not a few of our home staff are enjoying holidays this year through the thoughtfulness and generosity of friends who have offered their homes for this purpose. The Cornford House vegetable garden continues to flourish and its largesse runs over the wall as far as Sevenoaks, to the benefit of all of us in the office. At this time of harvest and fruitfulness, let us renew our thanks to our bountiful heavenly Father.

(GUY LONGLEY, UK HOME STAFF)

Chapter Five

SOMETHING TO SHARE WITH OTHERS

Missionaries, children and old age pensioners rise to the challenge of giving.

SHARING

I was amazed how well the pooling system works. Take for instance our board money. OMF makes a quarterly allocation of money for food according to funds available. During some quarters we may eat at "A" level or in leaner quarters at "C" level. Yet one look at my well-fed family will prove that no one suffers under this method. It is a comfort to know that my immediate supervisor as well as director eat at the same board rate as we do. This has forced us to budget, economize and act as careful stewards of the funds God has given.

Furniture and appliances are also pooled. When we moved out of our house in Central Thailand another missionary was able to use these things immedately. If there were no pool we would have had the headache of storing everything for a year.

During the last term we have proven the wisdom of the OMF pooling system. Not only is it a very cost-efficient way to run a mission, but it has a way of uniting the various missionaries on the field. If my brother or sister has few supporting churches and I have many, those extra funds do in effect go towards meeting his or her needs. Not only do we feel a part of a large family as we share the work, but in our frequent prayer meetings we can also share as a family in meeting our mutual material needs.

(LARRY & PAULA DINKINS, THAILAND)

INTO THE POOL

Not long after I had moved from Malaysia to the Philippines, I was very challenged by the General Director's article about "putting God to the test by giving to His work ourselves so that He can give more to us." At that time I was on the point of sending to the OMF General Fund some of the money which came from the sale of the little car I had used in Malaysia. The GD's word seemed to be the prod God saw I needed, so I went ahead and made arrangements for the transfer of the money.

Even before I did so, however, God was moving someone in the UK to send me a personal gift, which came through very soon after I had sent my gift. This person had never sent me anything before, in fact I don't know him very well, which made this experience even more precious. Soon after this a member of our church in Davao handed me a generous cheque, saying, "For a long time I have been meaning to give you this." Perhaps God was waiting for me to give more to His work first.

Yesterday we received notification of two very large personal gifts amounting to German marks 2900 (US$1,100). As the Easter holidays are approaching and the travel of our three children will be a personal expense, the thought could have slipped in so easily: "This is the Lord's provision!" However, we feel this amount should go to the OMF General Fund towards our support, and we trust we will still have just enough for the holiday travel in April. You can take this as "a testimony of the Lord's non-provision" by our choice, and we still praise Him.

Hearing the report on financial needs for the next quarter, I have been praying in regard to this and feel constrained to help.

I am not sure what I have in my account, being a rather poor bookkeeper! But please take fifty percent of

72

whatever is there and put it towards the greatest need for the coming quarter.

I received some personal Christmas gifts recently and I would like to ask you not to credit my personal account with the personal allowance next quarter. That is one way of sharing the Lord's blessing with the rest of the OMF family.

(FROM LETTERS TO OMF FINANCE DEPARTMENT, SINGAPORE)

WATER FROM BETHLEHEM

A lady wrote to us one day with this most unexpected gift. She lives on a council estate and has always had to be very careful in counting the pennies, even to the extent of not sending Christmas cards. Her letter said:

"I expect you remember that when you were preparing to go out to Singapore in 1963, I wrote to say that if you were ever in need you could come to us. Having given an invitation like that I felt I should prepare in some way financially just in case of need. So I took out an endowment insurance for one shilling and sixpence (before decimalization) per week for fifteen years. That time has now passed and the money has been paid out.

As things are now, with you and Michael married and having your family, and Ron and me preparing to exchange this house for a ground floor flat when the council has one empty, we could not put you up; only help in other ways.

Therefore, because the money was saved for the purpose of helping you, I have sent the eighty pounds to

73

headquarters to be transferred to your personal account, to use as you believe God would wish."

We have written to thank her and to say we cannot do other with this loving sacrifice than pour it out before the Lord, as David did with the water from Bethlehem's well.

On such sacrifical gifts does the Lord's work go forward. May He open the windows of heaven and pour out His promised blessings.

(MICHAEL & DIANA DUNN, INDONESIA).

SIMPLE-LIVING SUPPORTERS

A young bride-to-be wrote to inform the USA office that she and her fiancé had told their friends they did not want wedding gifts. Instead, they had asked them to give donations to OMF for the Lord's work.

One friend sent the UK office a cheque for £50, "instead of champagne at my daughter's wedding last Saturday", and thought others might like to follow suit! Another gift of £50 came from a young couple: the husband has a terminal illness and they had been given a gift for a new wheel-chair, but decided to pass it on for the benefit of the Lord's work.

One of our missionaries on furlough forwarded a gift with the following explanation: "Previously there were two sisters; one has now died. The remaining sister feels she must send as much as they did previously, and so she has had to rebudget for a smaller number of commitments. She has only her old-age pension, but the 'Jesus box' must come first. She didn't want to pay 28p for a postal order, so that is why I am forwarding the donation."

(STORIES FROM MISSION OFFICES)

FROM THE YOUNGER GENERATION

I was very encouraged a few weeks ago to hear from my mother that three children in her Bible Club (11 and 12 years old) had spent part of their holidays doing odd jobs so that they could send what they earned to me. Last week I received notification that £3 had been sent. I was really thrilled, especially as it was completely their own idea and done on their own initiative, and they are all from non-Christian homes.

(JEAN THOMAS)

One of the most encouraging letters to come to us over the Christmas holidays was one containing a cheque for £2.70. Two young brothers had tithed their Christmas gifts for the support of one of our missionary couples. How we thank the Lord for Christian parents bringing up their children in this way!

(FROM THE UK OFFICE)

Chapter Six

EXACTLY AS REQUESTED

God provides winter clothes in a black and white colour scheme, a Toyota Hiace van and six rolls of colour film exactly as requested.

FILMS WITH LOVE

Last month the first couple from Hong Kong were leaving for Orientation Course in Singapore, and I had been thinking about what kind of gift I could give them as a token of love. I know missionaries, especially new workers, always need to take photos, so I visited a few photo shops to check on the prices. They didn't have the kind of slide film I liked. I then thought maybe I should buy them colour print film instead, but I somehow ended up not buying any film at all.

The day of their commissioning service arrived and I still had not bought anything for them. So I decided to give cash as a love gift. Just a few hours before I went to the service I met a member of my church whom I had met only twice before, and to my great surprise he presented me with a gift. When I opened it I found, to my even greater surprise, six rolls of colour print film! How I jumped for joy!

The Lord knew my desire to share OMF family love with the new workers, and He also knew my limitations. I believe that He restrained my hands and feet from buying those films from the shops; then He stretched out His hand to plan this gift for me. Note the timing! Note the exact provision!

As I shared this with the new workers and with the friend who gave me these films, all of us could not help but praise and thank the Lord.

(ELEANOR TAM WORKS IN THAILAND.)

BLACK AND WHITE

Things aren't always "black and white". There was one year when the future looked uncertain and my life seemed to take on a very grey quality.

79

I had been accepted into OMF to do medical work in Thailand, but soon after this the door closed as the Thai Government was not allowing nurses to sit the exams to obtain work permits. So several months of waiting followed, as an appeal was made to the Thai government. I was glad of the time to be with my family again in Australia, after some years of living in the UK.

When it seemed unlikely that the policy would change, OMF suggested that I consider two openings in Japan. One was the position of Field Nurse, and the other the opportunity to be involved in nurses' evangelism. The offer of these appointments, a year after the door to Thailand had closed, seemed to be God's guidance to me to change direction to Japan, and my home church in the UK supported this. When confirmation came from OMF, the Lord's will at last seemed to be clear. My "grey" had changed to "black and white".

The Lord's provision, following His assurance that I should go to Japan, was also wonderfully "black and white". A kit for Japan was now needed ... but how to find clothes suitable for the snowy winter months which would greet me? The shops in the spring heat of Queensland were fine for buying a Singapore kit, but not for a Sapporo one.

My parents contributed the first item — a good suit from a Melbourne firm catering for overseas travellers. "Black and white — very smart," said Mum, obviously pleased. "Why not keep to the same colour scheme?" The season's colours should not have been too difficult to find, but after that wonderful beginning there was very little we could add to the kit. Finding winter clothes seemed impossible as the days grew hotter. And where to find a coat?

Some days later, Mum and I were trying in a large

store to choose a summer dress from among the many racks of them, when we heard an announcement above the hubbub. "Ladies — announcing our final winter stock clearance — these items are all reduced to $10." That magic word "reduced" attracted many others — but we managed to find two items of my size 10. Goodness! Black and white! Before we could pay for them came another announcement: "Ladies — a final reduction on these winter items — now $5."

"I'm going to live in Japan and thought it was impossible to get winter clothes now," I stumbled out to the salesgirl. "I'm sure people are praying about my shopping." Just as I finished, another salesgirl broke in.

"Excuse me. Would you be interested in this? Reduced from $100 to $20?" A black and white suit! Size 10! "It's imported and very warm." So off we went again to the fitting room. My mother thought it looked very special. "That acrylic fibre looks like silvery snow."

Some time later, my need of a coat was the only remaining concern. So far the only possibility seemed to be a sheepskin-lined one. My parents were very much in favour of my having the warmest coat available, as Mum had just been reading about migratory swans being frozen in the snow as they settled on the lakes of Hokkaido! My parents offered to buy me that sheepskin coat.

"They're so expensive," I thought.

"You'll be conspicuous, and that isn't advisable for a missionary," a Christian friend warned. She had been on a visit to Japan and found that the people dressed with uniform and conservative taste.

Then came the day when my father took me to a shop specializing in leather and suede goods. We had reached the deadline for finding a coat. I tried on one very stylish coat, but it was a size too small. The salesman wanted to arrange for the larger size to be brought from another shop that afternoon. What should I do? I remembered someone saying that they knew a lady who had been a missionary in Japan, and who now worked in the Baptist bookshop in the city.

"Lord, please guide," I prayed. "You see my parents' anxiety. We really need to know about this matter of a coat today." Then I phoned the former missionary, and enjoyed talking with her. It was twenty years since she'd been a missionary in Aomori!

"Advice on what coat to buy? Do you need one?" she asked. I learned she had just moved to Queensland from the colder southern states of Australia and had been planning for months to sell her heavy woollen coat.

"Would you like it? It's size 12, but you'll need plenty of room for layers. I'll drop it round. It's white.'

(JAN BRAY WORKS IN JAPAN.)

HEAVENLY MELODY

A whole chapter, if not a whole book, would be needed to tell of all the Lord did in connection with the six-week tour by Taiwan's Heavenly Melody Singers to South Africa and Zimbabwe in 1980. Here is just one example of God's provision.

We arrived home for our first furlough at the beginning of April that year, only two-and-a-half months before we were to welcome the Singers and accompany them on tour. These gifted young people were due to sing and testify for the Lord in such different places as tiny coal-mining Wankie and the gold-famous skyscraper city of Johannesburg. We were to share with them the awesome sight of the thundering Victoria Falls, as well as the kaleidoscope of ocean and mountain beauty along the Garden Route between Cape Town and Port Elizabeth.

However, as we pondered car prices in the papers and looked at those in second-hand car-dealer stands, we weren't sure just how we were going to cover all those kilometers. How could the two of us, the seven of them, and all the necessary luggage and equipment fit into anything drivable? We liked the look of the Toyota Hiace and told the Lord about it. However, we realized that such vehicles did not grow on trees, and the time for the Singers' arrival was approaching fast. Rev Louw of the Dorothea Mission had offered our Home Director the use of a VW Kombi for the first two weeks of the tour, but it looked as if we would also need to hire a van to carry all the equipment.

On the freezing southern hemisphere winter morning of June 24, 1980, the Singers arrived at Jan Smuts airport and later we all caught the airport bus to Pretoria, still not certain just what Rev Louw had been able to arrange. Imagine our feelings as we stepped off the bus to be told that the VW Kombi was not available — but quite unexpectedly a beautiful Toyota Hiace tourer was to be ours, free of charge for all the time we needed it!

That Toyota Hiace comfortably seated the nine of us with room for luggage (on the roof) and equipment (in the back). We travelled 9,000 kms during the next 45 days without a single flat tyre or breakdown. we had 60 memorable meetings, many with over 600 people in attendance and the largest with 2,000. Who can know the numbers, in both South Africa and Zimbabwe, of all races, who heard the Gospel and also the challenge of

Missions through the Singers? That Toyota actually belonged to a Christian choir whose director and her husband serve the Lord in Trans-World Radio. The Heavenly Melody Singers regularly make programs for beaming to Mainland China by, amongst others, Trans World Radio!

(PETER & GERALYN ANDERSON)

GOD'S TYPIST

A great deal of OMF work has been done over the years in New Zealand by volunteers. Their tasks include folding and enveloping magazines, acknowledging donors' letters, recording donations, pricing books and despatch of orders. When these jobs accumulate, the system becomes choked and the work slows down, but "many hands make light work" when several people can give a few hours once a week or so. Maud served in China and Malaysia but has since retired. For the past eleven years she has given at least a day a week to the Book Department, pricing, shelving, wrapping and cataloguing.

In 1973, when the Home Director's department was burgeoning with correspondence, there was not even a part-timer to assist. The need was made known to praying friends. At the same time a devoted Christian woman, who had recently retired from being a bank manager's secretary, sold her house in Dunedin and moved to Auckland. Challenged by Revelation 3:8, "I have set before thee an open door", she visited three adjoining missions in the building where OMF has its office and gave her change of address. While in the OMF office she was introduced to the Home Director, and not many days later she settled into her role as his typist. Since then, working on average three days a week for four hours a day, Mary has saved the mission upwards of ten thousand dollars.

(FROM THE NZ OFFICE)

Chapter Seven

EXACTLY THE RIGHT AMOUNT

God not only makes the gift match the amount needed but brings the price down to match the money available.

PURCHASE IMPOSSIBLE?

After Nongbua Christian Hospital had been handed over to the Government of Thailand and missionaries had been redeployed to other ministries, a further matter needed to be resolved. What were we to do with the OMF pickup vehicle that had been used at Nongbua?

It could, of course, have been sold to a dealer on the second-hand car market, but we prefered that it should continue to be used in Christian work, if possible.

After we had carefully assessed the different needs around Thailand, that of the Phayao Bible Training Centre stood out. The people there had a large truck for their dry-season evangelistic campaigns, but no smaller vehicle for weekend ministries or everyday use at the college. We inquired, and discovered that yes, indeed, they would like to have our vehicle. However, it was clear that their financial position made an outright purchase impossible. At the same time we felt it would not be right to give the vehicle to Phayao as a straight gift. This was not because we needed the money but rather that, as a matter of principle, the college should make some financial outlay.

The principal, Mr Somsak, was in Bangkok at the weekend when these discussions were being held. He asked, "Is it possible to have the vehicle? I could drive it back up to Phayao when I return on Tuesday."

I asked him, "How much do you need this vehicle, and can you afford to buy it?"

"We need it very badly," was his answer, "but you know that our finances do not really permit us to buy it."

We prayed and discussed it further, and finally the suggestion was put that we should sell it to them at half its market value. On the Saturday, Mr Somsak was

89

conducting the wedding of a former student, and after the ceremony a member of the congregation approached him. "Do you have any financial needs at Phayao?" he asked.

"Yes, of course we do," said Mr Somsak, but true to the spirit of faith he did not wish to be specific or to appear to be asking for finance. "There are many needs at the school," he said. "In fact, as the work advances, so do the financial needs." He thought no more about it.

The following day Mr Somsak was preaching at the church of a former student, and at the end of the service the man who had spoken to him at the wedding came up to him. "I'd like to give you a cheque," he said, "and it is for you to use at your discretion." To Mr Somsak's amazement the cheque was for the exact amount needed to purchase the pickup.

On the Monday, when he shared this with me, there were tears of joy in our eyes as we praised the Lord for His wonderful provision, and the faith and wisdom He had given us both.

(THAILAND AREA DIRECTOR)

GOD'S EXACT ACCOUNT

In February, an anonymous donor deposited 5,000 baht (US$218) into my Thailand account "for whatever usage is needed in the near future". I was quite taken aback at the amount but, as I was planning to fly to India to get married at the end of April, I thought that this would be the "usage", and assumed that the donor meant it for that purpose too.

However, my mother's health seemed to be deteriorating rapidly, and I had to fly to the UK instead and postpone the wedding indefinitely. Booking only two weeks ahead does not usually enable one to make travel arrangements at the cheapest rates, and so I anticipated that I would have to pay some of the fare home.

It was only when my statement arrived from Thailand some time later that I saw what had happened:

Actual cost of travel home– 17,000 baht
OMF travel allowance   – 12,000 baht
Difference   – 5,000

So God provided the exact amount before I even knew I needed it!

(DI CURRIE WAS EVENTUALLY ABLE TO MARRY THEO SRINIVASAGAM, WITH WHOM SHE IS NOW WORKING IN INDIA.)

GOD OF BETHEL

For some time we had been wanting to bring the Publications Warehouse in Sevenoaks nearer to the OMF Central Office, and to make adequate provision in one building for the whole of our Publications and Editorial Department. During February 1980 we began to recognize the urgency of this need, and an advertisement in the local newspaper one Saturday led us to inspect a detached brick property about ten minutes walk from our offices at Belmont, with a warehouse on the ground floor and offices on the first floor. The building, appropriately enough in a street named Bethel Road, had been completely refurbished just a year before, and the remainder of a 21-year lease was being offered.

The Home Director, the Publications Manager, the Editor and I gathered in the HD's office on returning from our visit to the building on Tuesday February 26, amazed at such a near-ideal provision, but wondering where the funds would come from. We knew that approval from International Headquarters in Singapore would be required and wondered if a capital sum could be set aside, the interest to provide sufficient income to cover the rental costs

While we were in the meeting, a gentleman called at the office and asked to see me. I came out from the meeting and found one of our most gracious and generous donors who had made the journey to Sevenoaks specially to tell me that he was planning to distribute the capital from his trust funds. He wished to make a large sum available to OMF on the understanding that it would be invested, with the interest to be used for whatever purposes we wished. I somewhat timidly asked him the sum he had in mind, and to my utter amazement it was exactly the sum we had calculated would be necessary to cover the cost of the new Publications building.

When I rejoined the meeting, we could do no other than stand in awe of what God was doing, and you will not be surprised to learn that the Singapore Directors echoed our hallelujahs! In all my experience of property miracles in the Fellowship, I cannot recall one quite as dramatic as this. Thanks be to God!

(GUY LONGLEY, UK HOME STAFF)

THE ROMANCE OF PROPERTY

The men who trudged the streets of Singapore in 1952, looking for suitable property for a mission headquarters and home, certainly did not find their task romantic — until God intervened in such a dramatic way that weariness and frustration were soon banished.

Following the withdrawal of the CIM from China, the new headquarters had been set up in a twenty-roomed boarding-house in Chancery Lane, Singapore. By this time the stream of returning missionaries was beginning to flow strongly and, before long, as with Elisha's school of prophets, the place was too small to accommodate them. So a search was instituted for more commodious and suitable premises.

The need for a permanent language school for those who were facing the challenge of entirely new languages and conditions added urgency to the search. If new office premises could be found, the Chancery Lane building lent itself admirably to the purposes of a language school.

Eventually an eminently suitable site was located, but the asking price was far beyond anything the Mission could afford. The property was situated in Cluny Road opposite Singapore's famed Botanic Gardens, and comprised two acres with a seven-bedroomed house and plenty of land on which to erect offices and flats. The airy living rooms of the house were ideal for a mission home.

Gifts were coming in, designated for new buildings in Singapore. But when tentative enquiries were made, it was discovered that the sale price of the property was Malay $170,000, more than twice as much as was in hand for the new headquarters. The desirable plot seemed unattainable, and yet, was this beyond God's power to supply? Prayer was constantly being made about the matter, and God was working.

One day the real-estate agent telephoned saying that he thought the owners of the property might sell for M$105,000 — a sudden drop of M$65,000! It was a most tempting offer, for the property was well worth the price originally asked. Had there been M$105,000 in the building fund, the offer would without a doubt have been readily accepted. But there was only M$85,000 available.

"We can give M$85,000 and no more for the property," said Rowland Butler, the Mission representative.

"I only have power of attorney to accept M$90,000," replied the agent.

It was no use. There just was not that extra M$5,000 in hand. The telephone receiver was replaced rather sadly. To be so near obtaining so eminently suitable a property, so urgently needed, and then to lose it just for lack of M$5,000!

But the transaction was still in God's hands, and the lack of M$5,000 was no problem to Him. He just brought the price down! The telephone bell rang less than five minutes later.

"Take the thing!" said a rather irate voice at the other end of the wire. "Take it for M$85,000!"

And so the money that had been coming in, much of it contributed by members of the Mission whose own purses were by no means overfull, proved sufficient after all.

There was another gracious evidence of a Father's overruling in this transaction. When the offices and apartment buildings were being erected on the newly purchased Cluny Road property, the block of land two doors away was also being prepared for the erection of apartments. Work began on both properties at about the same time, but the neighbour's property was found to require extensive and costly pile driving. It took them a whole year to lay the foundations alone. No piling was necessary on the Mission property, and all the buildings were completed before the foundations of the other building had been laid.

These offices and apartments have served the Mission well for over thirty years. Meanwhile the commercial centre of Singapore has been moving out towards the Botanic Gardens, and the property has multiplied many times in value. In 1982 a large commercial firm representing Middle East oil interests offered to buy the Cluny Road property for a price totalling millions of Singapore dollars.

With the transfer of the Orientation Course for new missionaries from the Chancery Lane property (now occupied by Discipleship Training Centre) to Cluny Road, the centralizing of the Fellowship's Communications Department in Singapore, and the creation of a Department of Home Ministries, the facilities are now stretched beyond capacity. The possibility of selling the Cluny Road property and developing new facilities in another location seemed attractive. After prayer and waiting on God, the Headquarters Directors were led of the Lord to reject the offer, believing firmly that just as God had so wonderfully provided the property more than thirty years ago, so today He is able to provide everything that is needed to redevelop the facilities according to present needs.

(FROM IHQ DIRECTORS)

PETROL IS
EXPENSIVE NOW

1973 went down in history as the year of the oil crisis. While Israel and Egypt went to war, the economy of the Philippines went crazy. From one day to the next prices doubled, and from time to time they went up another notch. When people asked incredulously why there was another price-hike of this or that, every vendor's stereotyped answer was "*Mahal na ang gasolina* — petrol is expensive now." The phrase became a grim joke whenever somebody lamented the horrendous price of rice, nails, or fares.

Our food allowance had been increased, but not in proportion to the price increases. We receive our allowance to cover three months at a time, and no one could have foreseen that prices would run away during that quarter. I began worrying. How could we survive? There was no way whatsoever to live decently on that allowance without overspending. Yet OMF principles say that we are not to go into debt.

I must confess that I started grumbling and, with every rise in prices, I grumbled more. "Didn't you pray in that situation?" you may ask. I couldn't see the use of it, since it seemed that prayer would neither increase my money nor decrease the prices ... So I worried on and looked for ways to cut down on expenses. However, with our frugal living there were no ways of cutting down left. The children needed their milk, rice and vegetables were essential, and protein had to be supplied also. I worked myself into a frenzy, of which I am ashamed to this day. I know that OMF would not have chided me if I had overspent during those months. But I somehow blamed the Lord for allowing such a situation to arise and for not keeping a firmer hand on the affairs of this country.

With clenched teeth I started doing our accounts at the end of the quarter. Now it would become obvious that the Lord had let us down, that He does not supply our every need ... I added and subtracted, going over the cash sheet again and again. But there it stood in black and white — the sum of all our expenses exactly matched the amount we had received ... right down to the last centavo. Never before (and never since) has this happened to us. A very humbled housewife had to ask for forgiveness for grumbling and unbelief.

(DORIS ELSAESSER, PHILIPPINES)

VISION AND SUPPLY

Flying home over Montreal for my first furlough, I glumly mulled over my past four years. Had God not called me specifically? Had He not sent me to South Thailand, His insistence and courage propelling me forward against my own natural reticence? Why then had He apparently not sealed His approval of my obedience by providing the needed financial support? How humiliating it seemed for me to be so dependent on others — I, who had earned my own way for many a year.

With such negative thoughts whirling around, I considered the future. Surely I should resign! Without the seal of His approval how dared I continue? Another colleague and I had prayed much together that God would give Christian friends the desire to share with me financially in the ministry at Saiburi Christian Hospital. Why had He not answered?

Bitterly I recalled the Home Director's questions during an interview four years previously. "How will you be supported?" he had asked. "Is your church firmly behind you in this?" His questions had brought me up short. Had I been presumptuous then in expecting my church family to stand with me financially? Most of them were not fully aware of OMF's policies, or of the fact that the Mission was only a vehicle for the churches for channelling to East Asia those who felt directed of God to serve Him in a cross-cultural witness there. Most of them didn't realize the OMF was cast upon God for the needs of each member, just like Hudson Taylor the founder, who received no supply except what God sent through His people.

Now, flying home from my first term of service, I faced the facts. Some in OMF received over and above what was needed to keep them each year. Their "extra" was helping provide for my lack, through the "pool" from which distribution was made equally to all. Without this policy I would not have arrived in South Thailand so quickly, nor would I have survived these past four years. But should I continue to live on others' supply, others' faith, draining the "pool" and not contributing anything to it from my own supporters?

As I fretted and even complained against God for breaking faith with me, I was hit with a question. It wasn't in audible words but it came clearly to mind nevertheless.

"How long, Roberta, did I wait for you to obey Me, to go and serve Me in Saiburi? Do you have no patience now while I give My vision to others to 'cowork' with you?" The rebuke hit home as I recalled my years of refusal to heed His promptings, and the years of His patience with me.

"Forgive me, Lord," I prayed. "It is your work to give the vision, for both vision and supply come from Your hand alone — and in Your time."

Since that momentous flight home in 1970, I have been humbled year after year as He has provided my support in full, despite recessions, the devalued dollar, inflation and the continual cry for funds by others in the face of worldwide need. He has supplied without fail,

98

without my asking except of Him, without friends knowing who else was giving or how much. Such is our God.

As I write the above, I have misgivings that some would search for a formula in this testimony. I can assure you there is none. It is not from great prayer or great faith but from the heart of a great and faithful God. I can only offer Him the deepest praise. Why He loves to be asked and trusted I don't undersand; to the fact that He does, I am only a witness.

(ROBERTA FRYERS, THAILAND)

Chapter Eight

EXACTLY AT THE RIGHT TIME

God's exact timing brings comfort, encouragement and assurance of God's will.

GOD WANTS IT
TO LOOK NICE

Just before Christmas 1979 I was praying one morning when the news in the letter I had just received began to sink in. Jean Barling, a fellow student from Ridgelands Bible College, was wondering about visiting relatives in Australia ... and about a possible trip to the Philippines on her way back!

Jean had spent the last five years as cook-caterer to the Archbishop of Canterbury, Dr Donald Coggan, at Lambeth Palace. He would soon be retiring and so would all his personal staff, including Jean. An opportunity for a long holiday ...? I knew Jean had been an interior designer employed by Heals of London before she had gone to Bible College, and ideas began to jump about in my mind.

Not long before, we had dug our first piece of turf on the lot the Philippines Home Council had bought for an office and mission home complex. The builders were begining to lay the foundations and I was beginning to realize my responsibility for the interior design! Could the Lord possibly so weave things together that Jean's planned trip to Australia sometime during the year would coincide with my need of help with decor, colour schemes and furnishings?

We experienced delays with the building right from the beginning. Electricity lines were slow in being connected, and it took so long to drill for water that all the cement had to be poured with water carried from our house. Eventually I heard from Jean that, after some delays of her own, she had made it to Australia. Her relatives wanted her to stay on and she was not at all sure when it would be appropriate for her to leave. We

103

weren't too sure, either, when we would be ready for her.

One day in mid July the foreman asked us for our choice of floor tiles and wall paint, and the next day a letter arrived from Jean saying she would be arriving in five days time. On her first morning we launched into plans, ideas and colour charts!

The next six weeks were full of hard work, invaluable help and corporate decisions — selecting combinations of soft, light colours, designing cupboards, searching out and ordering furniture, learning how to make old furniture look like new, choosing local fabrics for curtains and bedspreads — all in addition to the usual day-to-day running of the existing mission home.

To give Jean a glimpse of the Philippines outside Manila's shops, we took a short break in Calapan, Oriental Mindoro. But after we had been there for only three days a telegram arrived announcing that Jean's father was seriously ill, and she was needed at home to help her mother care for him. We returned to Manila and completed as much as we could before she flew to London three days later ... with much gratitude in both our hearts for what the Lord had given and for His perfect timing.

(SUE KIERNAN, PHILIPPINES)

ON TIME IN HIS TIME

I had a really beautiful experience with the Lord some years ago when I was in desperate need. I had 24 dental appointments within six months!

At first I went for only one visit, but this check-up

served to show me how much dental work I needed to have done. For six months I actually spent every Monday travelling up to Manila from Batangas City, several hours in the bus and then 15–30 minutes in the dentist's clinic.

I didn't mention to anyone my struggles over the finances for this, but I shared it with our heavenly Father, and He did a wonderful work.

God moved some godly men and women in Germany, people I didn't even know, to supply my big needs at that time. Through them as His instrument I was able to pay all the expenses, about US$360, from my own personal money, so that by the time of the last appointment I was able to pay the expenses without having any debt at all.

My superintendent asked several times whether I really had enough money to pay all these costs, and I told him honestly that God had provided on time, in His time. Praise His name.

(A MISSIONARY IN THE PHILIPPINES.)

PARTNERSHIP

"A partnership?" Surely my friend must be joking! But no, he was quite serious about my joining his accountancy practice after I had been less than one year in Canada. To work with him for a period and then eventually to take over the firm seemed almost too good an opportunity to miss — a God-given opportunity.

God-given? Perhaps. But within a few short weeks came the clear call of God to enter Bible College to prepare for full-time service overseas. I thought back over the past few years in Australia, when several close friends had left careers in business and professional life to train for Christian service. God's searchlight had turned on me at that time and, in an endeavour to avoid it, I had moved to Canada for further training. Now I was faced with the prospect of training for God's work, not exactly what I had planned! As I made plans to enter Toronto Bible College, I was glad that my accountant friend gave me his wholehearted support and was prepared to trust God to supply someone else to join his practice.

Six or seven years later, my wife Margaret and I were serving with OMF in Japan. One day a letter arrived from Don, another accountant friend in Canada, telling me that he had left a senior position with one of Canada's largest manufacturing companies, and was now without any prospect of another position. The Lord brought to my mind the offer that had come to me some years previously, and I wondered if my friend John was still seeking a partner and eventual successor. I wrote to suggest that Don should contact John, whom he already knew. How satisfying it was to learn some time later that my two friends were now in partnership, with John gradually moving out to a well-earned retirement!

Again the clock moved forward, this time to 1981, with Margaret and I and our four children based at OMF Headquarters in Singapore. Margaret had undergone major surgery for cancer followed by weeks of radiation therapy. In all she was hospitalized for six weeks, and the hospital bills, even with a generous "missionary discount", reached an imposing total. Finally her condition necessitated the immediate return of our family of six to Toronto. The travel costs, like the medical and hospital expenses, would not be paid by the Mission but were a personal responsibility. However would these be met? We remembered that God had promised to supply every need; indeed I had lectured to successive groups of new workers coming through the Orientation Course at Headquarters on this subject, assuring them that OMF's financial policy really works — God can be trusted. Had we not seen Him provide for the heavy expenses of the birth of three of our four children, in Asia where government-sponsored medical-insurance programs are not available.

God says that He is no man's debtor, and once again God proved Himself true as He moved to meet our financial need. Christian friends in Asia and elsewhere gave generously as they heard of Margaret's condition, but even their generosity did not match the expenses. Then one memorable day we received word of two cheques, sufficient to cover not only the airfares to Canada for the whole family but also for me to travel back to Singapore later in the year.

Before Margaret had been taken ill, I had been planning a business trip to the UK and North America. We had been trusting God to supply funds for Margaret to travel with me, and in anticipation of that visit Don and his wife had sent a gift of $1,000 towards her airfares. For some reason word of this gift had been delayed in reaching us, and arrived at the same time as news of Don's further gift of $5,000 towards the needs due to Marg's illness. The gift came at no small cost to Don and his family, but how we praised God for this wonderful "dividend" resulting from the decision I had made to follow God's path so many years before.

This special financial provision was representative of the countless ways that God supplied every need in the two and a half years that followed our family's return to

Toronto. The provision of housing, vehicle, holiday cottage, babysitters, housekeepers, meal makers, prayer warriors and a host of other supportive friends almost overwhelmed us. It was Don's wife who came to care for Margaret and our four children in the three weeks that I had to be away in Asia in September 1982, which turned out to be only shortly before Margaret's graduation to glory. As she left for home after that stay, Don's wife remarked, "You are surrounded by a cocoon of love in this place."

Truly, "God is able to do exceedingly abundantly above all that we ask or think." That verse, and the wonderful way in which we had experienced God's provision in so many areas, gave me courage as I faced up to the need to care for our four children without Margaret's counsel and help. The grief that came with her passing was mitigated by the knowledge that she was now free of pain and rejoicing in the Lord's presence. But how could God meet our family's needs for a wife and mother? I didn't realize it at that time, but in the months that followed I came to see that the family of my late friend Koos Fietje, murdered on the job as a missionary in Thailand, had a complementary need for a husband and father.

How Colleen and I thank God for the wonderful provision He has made for us in each other! What a joy it has been to return to Asia for a further period of service! A special bonus was a large gift towards our support just on the eve of our departure, a gift that covered fully the cost of travel to Singapore for our expanded family of nine. "My God shall supply every need of yours."

(ROB DAVIS IS DIRECTOR OF FINANCE & ADMINISTRATION AT INTERNATION-
AL HEADQUARTERS IN SINGAPORE)

GOD'S PERFECT TIMING IN THE PHILIPPINES

After I sent to International Headquarters in Singapore our first quarter remittance towards the support of the Maghirang family, our missionaries in Japan, there was almost nothing left in our account to meet the needs of the three families on home staff and furlough in the Philippines, and our administration expenses. It was only four days before the end of the month, the time when allowances are due to be paid. During the Council meeting when this was discussed, it was even suggested that perhaps we should not send anything to IHQ for the first quarter, because of the pressing needs on the homeside. But in the end we decided to remit US$500 (₱7,000) anyway, trusting that God would take care of the Home Council's daily needs. We prayed hard.

The following Sunday I gave a testimony at one of our supporting churches, and the leading elder told me that the previous day his company had decided to give us ₱15,000 (US$1,070), in addition to what we regularly receive from them. How I praised the Lord! But when I went to collect the cheque the next day, I found out that I was wrong. I had thought I heard ₱15,000, but it was ₱50,000!

(WILLIAM LAYDA)

During my first few months with Philippines Home Council as I was handling the cash and disbursements, I experienced the Lord's faithfulness in providing for the financial needs of His children.

At one time, three days before I had to give the Layda family their allowance, the balance was only about ₱138. During that time Mr Layda was out of

Manila and Mrs Layda and I were a little concerned what to do and where to get the money that we would need. I told Mrs Layda that we should wait and pray for the Lord's provision. The following day an envelope came with ₱2,000 in it, and a week after that we received, from an unexpected donor, an amount equivalent to US$2,000. That was the donor's initial gift which was followed at regular intervals by the same amount. This dear man's donation was pegged in dollars and so, with the continuing devaluation of the peso, the gift actually given in pesos had to be adjusted each time accordingly.

This is just one of many ways that we have experienced the Lord's provision and His perfect timing.

(LERMA RONQUILLO)

CAR ON OFFER

I had just returned to the UK from a month in Singapore, researching the feasibility of moving OMF publishing there. The next day my old car was due for its statutory test, and I was rather apprehensive about the result.

When I went to collect the car, the garage mechanic told me that, as I had half expected, it would cost a great deal of money to put right. What was I to do? It seemed likely that in six months or so I would be moving to Singapore — perhaps I could buy an "old banger" that would last me till then. Life without a car would be difficult to say the least, as I was living in a small village several miles from the OMF UK office where I worked. Distressed and confused, I called up Executive Secretary Guy Longley on the intercom from my office to his.

"What should I do?" I asked him. "Pay all that money to have it put right? Buy something old and cheap? I don't know much about cars and it's so easy to be cheated ..."

"Don't panic!" Guy told me. "Listen. We've just had the offer of a small car to be used by a missionary on furlough. Why don't you ring up the girl and ask if she'd be willing for you to use it for the next six months? You could pass it on to someone on furlough when you leave."

I talked to the donor immediately, and the next afternoon found me on the train to Oxford to collect the car. The timing was perfect, for she was leaving for a holiday that very night and had wanted the car safely gone before she left. It served me well for six months, and was used by several OMFers on furlough after that.

(EDYTH BANKS, COMMUNICATIONS DEPARTMENT, SINGAPORE)

"FOR YOUR CAR, WITH LOVE, ANON"

I had moved to a new locality, and was almost certain which church the Lord was leading me to join. But it would mean that I would need transport ... and for a single home staff member this was a financial impossibility. Kind people who lived in the opposite direction offered rides, but of course this wasn't always convenient.

Some years before, a friend had prodded me into opening a car account — but the balance in it was slender. Then, at about the time I was having to make a decision as to whether or not to undertake a specific ministry for which a car would be very helpful, this same friend handed me a cheque for a substantial amount. I was labelled, "For your car, with love, anon." She had no idea about the decision needing to be made.

Not long after this a suitable car was offered for sale, but then was unexpectedly withdrawn to be lent to furlough missionaries instead. Faith was tested, and I was uncertain because of this delay, but things were clarified when I was suddenly offered some petrol coupons by a caller to the office, someone who always gave anonymously. That seemed to clinch for me the fact that it was worth waiting God's time to see if this car would later become available.

Shortly after the petrol coupons were handed to me, I received the following unsigned letter from the person concerned, on a subsequent visit to the city.

"A few months ago I was left a small sum of money, a portion of which I felt was to be given back to the Lord. Never before have I been moved to make a personal gift to you, but in this instance your name seemed to come to the fore as if there was some personal need of yours. About the same time two petrol coupons were given to me, and these I placed in an envelope ready to post to you.

I did not know how to get the monetary gift to you anonymously, and eventually it was just bundled together with another small sum and the petrol coupons and the money given for the General Fund. But even when walking out the OMF office door I was prompted to stop and enquire whether you had a car, and to tell you the petrol coupons were for you. Even when taking the coupons out of the envelope, I still felt they should be left and the monetary gift added. Well, I just took the most convenient way of passing on this amount, but for the rest of the day and that evening was conscious that it should not have been done that way.

Enclosed please find your personal share of a gift

made to me. I thought perhaps the reason for the gift might be more important to you than the money itself, and couldn't find a way to do it anonymously."

The envelope contained $100 in notes!

How right she was! It was marvellous to be the recipient of this confirmation from the Lord, not only in regard to buying the much-needed car, the very one which had now become available, but as a seal on the steps I was taking to become a member of that particular church. The very real assurance that came through God's speaking right out of the blue to this person was intertwined with the guidance I was receiving through new circumstances.

(BETH ROOSE, NEW ZEALAND HOME STAFF)

LINKS ACROSS THE WORLD

In December 1979 I received a phone call from a pastor in Florida, saying that his church would like to send its Christmas offering to OMF for use among Cambodian refugees. He stipulated that the money was to be used for their spiritual well-being, not for their physical needs. When the money arrived it was $10,000. At about the same time a church in Birmingham, Alabama, was also sending a gift of $10,000 earmarked for Cambodian relief. These gifts were given before the prayer request for funding for Cambodian literature had even reached the States!

A few weeks before these gifts were received, a pastor had brought his flock out of Cambodia into the camp in Thailand in which Don Cormack was working. After this man regained his health and strength he began to preach the gospel, and thousands of Cambodians turned to Christ as a result.

So our loving Father was providing the literature needed for a church yet to be born, by prompting people half a world away to give, people who knew nothing of the circumstances in Thailand.

Subsequently, a number of these very Cambodians were resettled in Birmingham, Alabama, and are being taught and having fellowship in that same church which had given to them.

(PAUL HARRISON, USA)

Chapter Nine

FOR THOSE LEFT AT HOME

God's provision for parents who suffer separation from their loved ones on the mission field.

GOD CARES FOR OUR PARENTS

According to traditional Chinese culture, filial responsibility is extremely important, even for grown-up children. In Asia, where old people depend on their children for living, to discharge such responsibility is obligatory. We both grew up in Hong Kong and then, after study in Canada, became Canadian citizens. It was also in Canada that we became Christians and received God's call to be missionaries. However, it was several years before we went out as missionaries to Japan, and the chief reason for the delay was the fulfilment of this filial responsibility.

Yuen Ling is the third of four daughters, and since there was no boy the whole burden of supporting her parents fell on her. Shortly before we were married, her parents migrated to Canada to live with her. They were not Christians and had no sympathy towards Christian ministry. Although we were conscious of the call to be missionaries, at that time we were unable to follow the call for this reason. We spent much time in prayer, but doubt and frustration often prevailed. Eventually we felt that we needed to step out in faith, taking practical steps to become missionaries and trusting that God, in His sovereign way, would either open or close the doors for us. Shortly after we made application to OMF, a series of things happened that showed indeed God's guidance and provision.

The first was that Yuen Ling's father passed away. During his week in hospital he repented and believed in the Lord and so we, though grieved, rejoiced that he was in the Lord's presence. Yuen Ling's mother was very shocked, and felt very insecure and even more attached to us than before. We had great difficulty in attending

117

the OMF Candidate Course in Canada, but even so we felt that God was working out a solution for us. We prayed that God would change Mother and open the way. In a miraculous way God did work, and within six months Mother's attitude changed greatly.

A friend of Yuen Ling's mother, who had been a Bible woman in China, gave her a lot of encouragement and moral support. As a result of this, she consented to our going to the mission field on condition that we guaranteed her a monthly income to cover all her expenses. At that time the only asset we had was a condominium. We had about three months in which to sell it if we were to attend the June Orientation Course in Singapore, and we needed a cash offer for it rather than mortgage payments, in order to support Yuen Ling's mother. This was soon after the Iran-American crisis, when the economic situation was chaotic. Interest rates were very high, making a cash offer very unlikely, and condominium sales were in a slump at that time. So we really needed a miracle from God.

For two months or so only a couple of people came to see our place, none of whom seemed to be a prospective buyer. Then a young single girl came and gave us a cash offer of the exact amount we had prayed for. We could hardly believe that such a large amount of cash would come from a young girl! But just before the end of February the transaction was completed. *Ebenezer* and *Jehovah Jireh* be praised! So we were full of praise and joy when we set out for Japan in June 1980.

In these past years we have continued to see God's grace to us, especially in the area of finance. Basically Yuen Ling's mother lives on the bank interest, but because of inflation we have to supplement this every year. We had some savings in our account before we left

Canada, and so far we have been able to send her what she required — over 70 percent of the remittance we receive from OMF — and still find that we have almost the same amount or even more left in the bank. It is wonderful to see how God provides, and we believe that He will continue to provide for our mother in the future.

(GEORGE & YUEN LING YIP)

"LONGING TO SEE YOU"

My home is in Northern Ireland, where my 74-year-old mother and three younger brothers still live, but for the past 17 years I've been working in Indonesia, where there are abounding opportunities for serving the Lord. When I was about one-and-a-half years into this term of service, I was greatly surprised to receive a phone call from our Director, asking if I would be interested in a trip home that year. A gift had been received to help pay the fare for a single missionary.

I gasped for breath, and requested a day or two to think about it. Many questions went through my mind during the next few hours. What about the balance of the fare needed? What about the US$215 exit tax from Indonesia? What about the two other single women in this field whose need to see their parents was greater than mine?

The next day I had a letter from my mother informing me that £200 had been paid into my homeside account, and this news gave me the assurance that I should go ahead. It was as if the Lord had sent two ravens to make sure I got the message! Then I asked our Director about the other girls, and learned that for various reasons neither of them could go at that time. My mother's reaction further confirmed things. She said, "For the past two weeks I've had a longing to see you!"

So we do thank and praise our heavenly Father who cares for all sorts of needs, "over and above". One other bonus was that I was able to be present at my brother's graduation from London Bible College. He is now also an OMF missionary.

(MARGARET YOUNG)

THE CONSEQUENCES ARE GOD'S RESPONSIBILITY

Towards the end of 1973 I knew that soon I had to take definite steps towards full-time service, in response to God's call. But I was concerned for my family. Their support weighed heavily on my heart, as I was the main breadwinner then. My younger sister requested, "Sis, could you wait for another year so that I can take up a year of commercial study?"

I felt this dilemma very keenly. Here were two equally legitimate demands, my responsibility to my family and my obedience to God's call. What was I to do? God answered me in this situation in the words spoken to Hannah in 1 Samuel 1:23: "Do what seems best to you, wait until you have weaned (her); only, may the Lord establish His Word."

During that year of waiting, as my younger sister prepared herself for a career, I saw her also growing in maturity to the point where she would be able to take responsibility for the family and give both financial and emotional support to our parents.

As I entered Bible College in January 1975, it

became urgent for my younger sister to secure a permanent job so that she could take over this role as supporter of the family from me. Many friends were praying for us both at that time. She went for an interview and was put on a short list of two. Although she had minimal qualifications and no work experience, she was given the job.

I have learned two important lessons through these experiences. One is that God is responsible for the consequences of my obedience. For me this meant the possibility of hurting my mother deeply and leaving her in a state of seeming despair. This was very hard for me to take, but the Lord gave me peace. Secondly, I had to learn that no one is indispensable — not even me!

Over the years God has remained faithful to us as a family, binding us brothers and sisters together in our care and concern for our parents, supplying our every need (which is not the same as every luxury!), and giving us contentment with His providence.

Recently the mission chairman of my home church wrote to me after he had visited my mother: "I thank God who favoured me enough to enjoy the privilege of having fellowship with your mother on January 4th. She is looking well and ever praising God for His providence and care. Your younger sister and brother have been extremely supportive and caring towards her. Praise God! During my hour-long chat with her, all I heard from her was words of praise and honour to God. What a great testimony!"

(CHEONG SOH LIM, FROM SINGAPORE, IS NOW WORKING IN THAILAND)

FAMILY REUNION

In November 1982 I sat dejectedly thinking about my brother's wedding, only two months away.

How could I, a Malaysian, be absent from an occasion like that, which would be a family reunion too? But my Australian husband and I were working in Lawas, in East Malaysia, and the wedding was to be over in Peninsular Malaysia. According to OMF procedure, we can visit family only during our four-week holiday each year. So it seemed totally impossible. What could I do but seek God's will in this matter?

Suddenly one day our language supervisor said to us, "I think it would be best for you to spend another couple of months doing language study in Kuala Lumpur. And since you're going to be over in Peninsular Malaysia anyway, you could attend your brother's wedding." I could hardly believe my ears!

My family was overjoyed to see us, and my father was praising God the whole time. I even had the privilege of leading a prayer during the marriage ceremony. There were many other benefits from this visit too. The reunion deepened our family relationships and my husband's sensitivity to Asian ways was highly respected. We had many opportunities to share with people about OMF and about the work we hoped to do. As well as this, just as we arrived our small daughter proved to have impetigo, and she was able to get good treatment from a skin specialist. So we praised God for going before us in every way. We acknowledged Him, and He made straight our path, as Proverbs 3:5-6 promises.

(SHAMINI HAVERFIELD)

CAST ON THE LORD

During 1977 we experienced that the Lord can supply big needs as well as small ones. At home a family problem had erupted and we felt constrained to take six months leave-of-absence back in UK. We had sufficient funds in hand for the trip home, but were cast upon the Lord for our support during the months there.

Shortly after our arrival, the postman brought a letter in an unfamiliar handwriting, and out dropped a cheque for £500. "I have been receiving your prayer letter for many years but you haven't often heard from me," ran the letter in a shaky elderly hand. "Recently I retired from medical practice and received a special bonus. The Lord has guided me to send the enclosed cheque to you." How we praised the Lord for this — the biggest single gift we had ever received.

Another friend had been saving up to have her car repaired but found that need supplied from another source, so gladly sent us a gift. Other friends sent smaller gifts and some brought food. We were amazed to witness the Lord's hand in moving His children to be generous, and together with our friends we rejoiced in His goodness.

(MAY JOHNSTON, EAST MALAYSIA)

Chapter Ten

FOR THE FAMILY

God's special care for missionary families extends to providing houses, stand-in grandparents and school fees.

Our Times in His Hands

We were feeling limp after three years in our little Malaysian village, battling to feel we belonged in an alien culture, sweating six hours a day on Cantonese language study and trying to bring up our two small children in a setting where standards were all different from our own. The humidity didn't help. Just once I had resorted to wearing a light cotton short-sleeved cardigan, but for the rest it was the lightest summer wear all year round — and still we dripped. We were limp and we admitted it. We knew the Lord was with us but the joy was just not there.

Everything seemed to be piling up against us. I had had two miscarriages and was finding it hard to recover any spring in my step. Just then a sort of gold rush hit our village. A valuable mineral sand had been discovered in the soil of the village creek bed and everyone was going wild scrabbling in the mud for that extra dollar. Our very efficient fourteen-year-old house girl was swept up in the rush of instant wealth and left us for greener fields. The price of househelp skyrocketed overnight and priced us right out of the market. That meant that tasks such as carrying water from the well, sweeping up the cockroach droppings from the atap roof of our house, and ironing with the charcoal iron were added to our list of chores.

It was just then that I discovered I was pregnant. This one had to be carefully nurtured. The doctor's advice was brief: "Go home and stay there until you are 20 weeks. Don't even come and see me!" I hadn't expected anything quite so drastic and I found the narrow confines of village life very constricting during the next five months. "Well," I countered, "at least I'll

127

have plenty of opportunity to press ahead with my second-last language exam." But nevertheless, now that I could no longer go to nearby Kuantan town every so often, life was a very routine affair. We learned to create our own fun, and I was beginning to love the local women, although I did not always appreciate their feeling my growing tummy and sagely predicting that it would be a boy because my tummy was pointy, or that it was a girl because I was carrying it so high. They were kindly in their intent, and I was glad that they felt so much at home with me. Wouldn't it be lovely when my language was good enough for me to feel really at home with them!

With all that going on, it seemed the right moment for a letter home to our prayer partners. We bared our hearts to them, telling that we were finding the going tough and that our spirits seemed as listless as our bodies. Little did we know that our heavenly Father was preparing so many good things for us, things that were to enrich us until this day.

The first came in a letter from Val, a distant acquaintance in Australia. She had seen our circular and was writing to ask if she could become a special prayer partner, just for the time until our furlough. She wrote, "I am recovering from surgery and, as I lie in bed, I have so much more time to pray than I usually do. So I asked the Lord whom I should pray for, and I am sure He guided me to your letter. I sense that you are in particular need right now. Please allow me to share it with you. If you write frequent little notes telling me of particular needs I will be able to pray very especially for you as a family." How we thanked our loving Lord for this assurance of His loving care, and for people like Val. We were so encouraged to press on. We were frequently in touch with Val in the ensuing months and I believe we were mutually enriched as we all saw the Lord honour His promise to answer all those who call upon Him.

As furlough approached, my very down-to-earth, practical husband was already looking toward furlough meetings and the practical preparation for them. He had already been busy with his camera, and had perfected the art of copying slides, but now he was concerned that the meetings be well prepared and well conducted. He hated the idea of depending on uncertain equipment made available by different churches as he moved around. As we talked about it together we felt the Lord was guiding us to trust Him for the money to buy a projector before we left Malaysia, where prices were cheaper. But in order to avoid Australian import duty, we would need to have owned it for six months before we arrived home. The only option was to buy it almost immediately out of everyday personal funds, and trust the Lord to send us money later to cover the amount. Were we being rash? John especially felt that God was guiding him to buy the projector immediately, and so we did so. I had my little quivers of doubt, but John was steady in his certainty and I sheltered under that. In the months that followed we received no large spectacular gifts — we never did. However, when we balanced our budget at the end of the quarter, we saw that from here and there, in little gifts from near and far, the exact amount for the projector had come to us. We quietly praised the Lord for His guidance and His provision.

We were concerned also that our furlough clothing allowance had not arrived. I badly wanted to get some clothes made for the children before we left our village with its cheap dressmaker. I also knew that as soon as the baby came I would have to stay at home for a month according to Chinese custom, and would not be able to go out shopping. Unless the allowance arrived before the baby did, I would not be able to go to the shops to buy material. We were due for furlough a month after the baby was due, and so timing was rather tight!

We knew that others going on furlough at the same time as us had received their allowance long before. Had the Singapore OMF office just made a mistake? Should we write to them and query it? But the people in the office were so efficient that we hesitated to do that. Anyway, didn't our heavenly Father know our needs? Couldn't we trust Him and capitalize on yet another opportunity to prove that He would meet our needs as we committed them to Him in simple trust? It seemed better that way. It could be a growing experience. So we daily prayed that OMF in Singapore would remember the Timms' clothing allowance, and daily nothing happened, and daily my due date crept closer. I did my language exam, my due date came and went, and still there was no money. I drafted out patterns, worked out yardages and was all prepared for a shopping spree, but had no wherewithal to shop ... no money and no baby.

Then one day John bounced in through the door, waving a cheque with an enclosed letter from Singapore apologizing for the oversight. What a lovely moment of worship that afforded! Later that same day a very pregnant Australian woman was seen carefully choosing all sorts of materials in a shop in nearby Kuantan, and then later she was seen at the village dressmaker's, handing over materials and instructions. That same night, two weeks overdue, our baby started to clamour for her place in the sun. The next day Heather was born! Didn't the Psalmist say, "Our times are in thy hands?"

Heather's arrival was accompanied by another little miracle. We had wondered how I was to get to the hospital when the time came, for it was twenty miles away. When Philip had been born three years earlier, we had swapped houses with the two lady missionaries living in Kuantan. But that had been a lot of inconvenience for everyone and we really didn't want to do it again. We prayed, and sensed that God's guidance was to stay put and trust the Lord to overrule. If I had to go in the daytime, there was a bus or perhaps I could even get a seat in a passing taxi. Of course if it was in the night ... that did pose problems. We were quietly confident that the Lord would order all our ways, and we thanked Him for His peace. What we did not know was that when Heather chose to arrive it would be a midnight dash in a brand new car the Lord was to provide for us.

A teacher friend in Kuantan was learning to drive, and decided to put in her order early for the particular car she wanted to buy — a Hillman Imp which had to be mid-blue with matching upholstery. The Hillman agents in Penang said she would have to wait, but that posed no problem as she still did not have a licence. But then, to her surprise and consternation, the agents rang a day or two later to say that a car of that exact specification had arrived unexpectedly, and they were sending it over straight away.

"Goodness me," panicked Lillian. "What will I do? I can't drive yet."

Her mind ranged over the different people she knew and the Lord guided her to think of us. "Yes, John Timms is just the person. He is so handy with cars. He will look after it well for me and run it in for me too. I wonder if he would mind?"

She needn't have worried — we were ecstatic. The

131

Lord had quite clearly guided us in our praying and Lillian in her thinking.

Thus, parked in our little lean-to shed next to our crude village house, was a new mid-blue Hillman car (with matching upholstery), all ready for our moment of need. I shall never forget the sheer joy of waking up to those first birth pangs, tumbling into the little car and purring off into the night. As we crossed the Kuantan bridge, dawn was breaking, and we sang and praised the Lord together for His goodness. It seemed as though those morning shafts were literally reaching out and embracing us, and telling us yet again that His faithfulness is new every morning.

(JOHN & BLODWYN TIMMS, AUSTRALIA)

A PLACE FOR THE FAMILY

David and Roslyn Hayman, missionaries in Japan, had asked us to find them a furnished house somewhere in Sydney for six weeks during December 1982 and January 1983. They wanted to spend these precious weeks of holiday with their five boys, who ranged in age from 13 to 23. "It would be nice if it were near the sea," David had said. This was a tall order and we hardly knew where to start.

David's brother Theo decided that at least he could put a notice of the need in his local parish paper on Sunday. On that same day a Christian family were unable to attend their own church and went to Theo's church instead. They saw the notice in the paper and, as soon as the service was over, went to Theo and offered their house for the six weeks the Haymans needed it, as they were going to be away for that period.

The house was big enough to be convenient for David and Roslyn's large family. It wasn't near the sea — but it did have a swimming pool!

(ROY FERGUSON, AUSTRALIA HOME STAFF)

FAMILIES — A HUNDREDFOLD!

One of the exciting facts of our missionary life has been moving. CIM was described as Constantly In Motion, and OMF follows this tradition as Only More Frequently.

For our family this has meant leaving the comfortable womb of North America and exploring rural Thailand, Bangkok's snarled traffic and Singapore's cosmopolitan luxury. Tossed into the adventure have been treks to primitive tribal homes, dinners with Prime Ministers and royalty, tears of taming a tonal language, white-knuckled *betjak* rides beside Jakarta's not-so-fragrant canals, and snorkel dives with sharks.

All this may sound very exhilarating, but there are other aspects. We expect life's usual blend of joys and sorrows, but missionary life often has one inherent problem.

It's like this. We have two wonderful sons. Children need grandparents and our boys have two sets of the finest made. However, they have never lived within two thousand miles of each other! When our two sons were seven and five years old, we moved to Robesonia in Pennsylvania to prepare for the relocation of OMF's USA headquarters from Philadelphia. Nestled in beautiful, fertile, Pennsylvania Dutch country, Robesonia seemed like a whole new world. The basic conservatism provided a solid ethos for raising the boys, but making new friends was not going to be easy, so everyone said.

OMF has a strong family spirit among its members and supporters, which has been a deep comfort to many far from home. Our boys had "aunts" and "uncles" scattered all over the world. Still we felt, and God knew, that the boys needed that spiritual reinforcement and model outside the "inner circle". We prayed specifically that God would bring our lives into harmony with those special people who could minister to us in that way.

It wasn't long before Faith "happened" to meet an open, warm-hearted lady in a home Bible study group. Then we met her jovial husband at the little church we decided to attend. Before long we were invited to their home for supper and almost spent the night! Ray and Edna Staller, who became our boys' "Dutch" grandparents, had five children of their own, though only two teenage boys were still at home. The Staller home was wide open to everyone. The coffee was always hot, and Edna cooked teenage-boy-sized meals with plenty of pie, cake and cookies to fill in the chinks. The Stallers lived on a large farm with two ponds hiding big, hungry bass, and surrounded by fields providing pheasants, squirrels and ground hogs. This dreamland was tucked away into some beautiful hills only five miles from home.

What more could we want? We could pile out of the car any old time and be accepted, warmly hugged, listened to and even appreciated. Yes, there was one more thing. Both Ray and Edna had a deep love for our Lord. The years ahead were to hold many precious times of Bible study, church activities, heart-to-heart talks and prayer. God knew our boys' need. He also knew Faith's and my need for His promised family-away-from-family. His provision was abundantly above what we had asked or thought.

Ray and Edna are just two of the many "relatives"

God has provided for us over the years. None of His provision is deserved, but His mercy fills our hearts with comfort and encouragement as we now live in Singapore and the boys are making their own ways in America. He is faithful in the way He keeps on providing.

Guess what! We've just found the neatest family to be "aunt" and "uncle" for!

(STU & FAITH IMBACH, COMMUNICATIONS DEPARTMENT, SINGAPORE)

HOUSES – A HUNDREDFOLD!

Jesus promised "houses" in Mark 10:30 and we've proved that to be true.

With furlough coming up in 1978, we wrote to Brian Dean, our OMF Regional Secretary in England, saying that, as all our children were now located in the south, we would need to rent a furnished house in that region, preferably near the school three of them were attending.

The very same day that Brian received our letter, a man came into his office and said, "I've been posted to Belgium for three years. Would any of your missionaries be interested in renting our house in Camberley, Surrey?"

"Yes indeed," said Brian, "I have a letter right here inquiring about housing in the south. How much rent would you charge?"

"Does the Fellowship make a rent allowance?" he asked.

"Yes, £15 a week."

"Right, we'll call it that."

So we went to live in a beautiful, five-bedroomed home, ideally situated close to the school and to Guildford, where our daughter was nursing.

Four years later we needed once again to locate a suitable furnished house for renting. We flew home from Thailand without a clue as to where we would live, and expecting five children to descend on us for Easter in a few days time! At the airport our nephew, who was meeting us, told us that a phone caller that very morning had mentioned a possible house. Next day we gazed in wonder at a delightful five-bedroomed house, with everything provided. It was being offered to us for the current Fellowship rent allowance of £25 a week, in spite of having a market value of £150 a week. The owner had left just the previous Saturday for a year in Sabah.

Our kids are all very keen on sports and so they were specially thrilled that the tenancy included the use of a tennis court, squash courts, and a boating lake. Yes, God gives a hundredfold. But perhaps the most precious provision of all was the complete peace in our hearts as we journeyed home, proving Philippians 4:6-7 as well.

(JIM & DOREEN TOOTILL, THAILAND)

GOD'S MIRACLE HOUSE

"Looking for a home in British Columbia!" exclaimed our friends. "At the cost of homes today you haven't a chance."

Since returning to Canada from a short time of service in the Philippines, we had found it hard to remain in any house for very long. Either the rent was too high or the landlord wanted to sell, and so we had to keep moving from place to place. We ended up in a two-bedroom apartment, with one bedroom being used as an office. For $600 a month, we felt we were spending too much of the Lord's money for so little. Then we heard that the owner was going to increase the rent considerably.

"Our God is still a God of miracles," we reminded one another. "We shall look to Him for a miracle." We asked friends to pray for a home for us, but they just told us it was impossible. We went to inspect houses ... and we kept praying.

While we were at an OMF prayer conference in Victoria, a lady came and told us she had a home she would like us to view. Not wanting to offend her, we made an appointment to see it the following Monday morning.

Our first reaction when we saw the house was to look at one another and say, "We could never afford anything like this!" It was beautiful — a large 14-roomed house, close to the sea and to a lovely park. Its furnishings were antique, and as the lady took us round she pointed out various items of furniture and household equipment that would go with the house.

As we began to discuss business, Doug shared OMF's financial policy with her, telling her we live by faith and do not go into debt. "What is the price?" he asked her.

"Oh, Mr Shortt," replied the lady quickly, "we aren't asking you to buy the house. We want to give it to you!"

We soon discovered that this beautiful house had for forty years been the home of the Rainbow Christian Fellowship, a Christian welfare organization for girls. As this work had closed down, the people responsible were obeying God's call to pass on their home to another group of His servants.

Now it holds two suites in which two retired missionary families are living, and it has also been a lovely home for us.

How we praised the Lord for His provision, and how amazed were our friends who had told us it was impossible!

(DOUG & IRENE SHORTT, CANADA)

... AND HOUSE BUYER

During the fall of 1981 and well into the summer of 1982, the housing market throughout Canada ground to a halt. High interest rates had pushed the mortgage rates out of reach for most folks. More and more people had to put their homes up for sale, while few could afford to buy new ones. In Brantford, every third house seemed to have a FOR SALE sign on display. And here we were, needing to sell our house urgently, so that we could move to Fredericton on July 1st to join the OMF home staff there.

Two months passed with no buyers. Then, one evening in June we called a family prayer meeting, and asked the Lord to "send us a buyer *now*."

While Oliver was still praying, the phone rang. "Can we come now to look at your house?"

They came, they looked, they came again — and they signed the contract just two weeks before we had to move out. Thank you, Lord!

(LOUISE HARWOOD, CANADA)

CAN WE AFFORD KINDERGARTEN?

After we joined OMF, we experienced many changes in our financial situation. As a Korean pastor, I had received a regular monthly salary, but in OMF the amount received may be different every quarter. We began to worry about the exchange rate of the Korean *won* and about the different prices in each country. Then too, people in Korea thought that because we were in an international organization we would receive a lot of foreign money! When we left Korea, we were planning to go to Thailand, and so we didn't take anything except summer clothes and books. While we were at Orientation Course in Singapore our designation was changed to Japan, and we found that our personal allowance was not enough to buy winter clothes along with all the household things we needed.

But our Lord knew what we needed. We arrived in Japan in December, when the winter was very cold. Almost every night our fellow-workers brought us clothes and various household things, and once someone said, "I don't know why at this time a lot of things are coming into the OMF office. Maybe it is for the Byuns." I am sure our faithful Lord provided for us.

It was ten months after leaving Korea that we finally arrived in Japan — because of English study in Australia and visa changes in Singapore. All that time we did not receive any personal gifts from Korea, because people didn't know how to send money to us. We knew OMF's financial policy and so we couldn't ask for what we needed. When our fellow-workers received personal gifts, frankly sometimes we felt envious.

Just before our first summer holiday in Japan, when our son Miral was four years old, we decided to send him to a Japanese play-school. We tried a nursery school where working mothers receive financial help, but the Japanese Government didn't agree that Ae Ran was a working mother. They thought that being a full-time language student wasn't working! We felt then that a government-supported school was not the Lord's will, and prayed about a regular kindergarten, but we knew that there was no way except through prayer. Usually new students are accepted only in April, and it was already August.

Ae Ran decided to visit the principal of a local kindergarten, and found him exceptionally warm and nice. He said that actually they could accept students anytime, and then told Ae Ran that he would waive the entrance fee of ¥70,000 (about US$300), which still left us the monthly fee of ¥20,000 (US$85) to find. Then he admitted to Ae Ran that he had attended church with his uncle when he was a child. Later Ae Ran had more discussions with this principal about Miral, and he told her he used to attend an English Bible study that was taught by an OMF lady from Switzerland. Ae Ran was very excited, because it seemed that we reminded him of the fellowship he had once had with another OMF missionary.

Just before we actually left for our holiday, we received a letter from one of our prayer companions with a personal gift. This friend wanted to send regular personal support for Miral's kindergarten fees!

(JAE CHANG & AE RAN BYUN)

GOD'S TELEPHONE

We were home on furlough from the Philippines, and during our children's school holidays we spent a few days at the guest house of our former Bible school in Switzerland.

One lunch-time our companion at the table was one of the Bible school staff. Our conversation centered around that favourite theme: the schooling of our three children. Sending children to boarding school at the tender age of six is something completely alien to Continental minds. More often than not, we had to defend our actions and explain endlessly why this was the best solution. But maybe criticism helped us to cope better with the problem of separation from our dear ones than sympathetic compassion would have done.

However, this time we were talking to an understanding father who was ready to discuss the needs and problems connected with schooling. We explained the new step of faith we and the OMF had taken just recently: our own mission school in the Philippines had ceased operating in favour of sending our children to the German School in Singapore which also included high school. OMF would operate a hostel from which the children would commute daily. We explained that this school was very expensive because, although it received some subsidy from the German government, it depended mostly on school fees for operation. Nearly all the 200 students were the children of business people whose companies shouldered these expenses, but OMF was not a wealthy company, and it weighed heavily on our minds that to educate our children would cost more than to keep us parents on the mission field!

This was about as much as we felt free to share. We did not mention that we had asked the Lord to give us some sign that He would provide the school fees — that we were even considering staying at home if there was not a strong indication from the Lord that He was in control of our financial needs.

The dining-hall was crowded and buzzing like a beehive, with lively conversations around each table. Yet had somebody been eavesdropping on our discussion? Had we talked too loudly? We will probably never know. But the Holy Spirit must have been working overtime, and somewhere near us there must have been a person with a fat wallet, a love for the Lord's work and a heart sensitive to the Spirit's prodding. Since we knew that our conversation partner did not have a fat wallet, we were pretty sure he was not the one. But at supper-time we discovered an envelope on our place at the table. It contained SFR2,300 (US$1,060) and a printed note: "For the schooling of one of your children."

Another incident involves a church whose minister was a faithful friend of ours. It was the custom of his denomination to set aside a certain portion of the offerings for missions. Our friend was not very happy about the job some of their mission boards were doing, and so he and his congregation decided to send their offering to OMF for our support. For six years this became an annual event, to which we looked forward with grateful hearts.

Then our friend turned 65 years old, which meant retirement. His successor, who didn't know us, promised to continue with the tradition, but a year passed and no gift arrived. Had he forgotten his promise? Should we remind him? We knew the money was there, just waiting to be channelled to the right place. We decided to pray and trust God to remind them. Wasn't He completely capable of doing just that? But nothing happened, and as the weeks turned into months it was sometimes difficult to resist the temptation to send a reminder. But we hung on. After ten months we finally heard from them: the church had discovered its omission and was sending its contribution for the previous and the current year in one amount. The Lord's telephone had been working!

(DORIS ELSAESSAR, FROM GERMANY)

GREAT IS THY FAITHFULNESS

When we went home to the Philippines for furlough in 1978, our daughter Eunice was just finishing twelfth grade through an American correspondence course. She finally received her high school diploma three months before we were scheduled to return to Japan for our third term, and we were suddenly confronted with the problem of her college education. OMF provides for the primary and secondary education of its missionaries' children, but this provision normally ends when children turn 18. We were certain that the Lord wanted us to return to Japan, but we were uncertain what to do with our daughter, who was already over 18 years old. In the Philippines it is not possible to study and work at the same time, as 18-year-olds do in some western countries. So we felt that we could not leave her on her own.

Before we returned to Japan, our daughter applied for student aid from Bryan College in Tennessee, USA, through the recommendation of a friend who had graduated from that college. She was actually granted a tuition scholarship, because the college thought she was an American citizen, but later she was informed that she could not, after all, be granted such a scholarship because it was federally funded. This news came as a big shock to us, but we were reminded of the words of Paul in 2 Corinthians 4:8: "We are perplexed and unable to find a way out, but not driven to despair ..." After much prayer, we decided to take our daughter back to Japan with us, even though we had to pay for her travel expenses. We hoped that she would be able to teach English and thus save money for a college education.

After we had been in Japan for a few months, Eunice was able to obtain some English teaching, but for only two hours a week which did not really help her much financially. However, at about the same time we received a letter from an elderly lady who was working in the office of Bryan College in the United States. This kind Christian lady had noticed our daughter's application from the Philippines, and in His own time the Lord laid a real burden upon her heart to help Eunice go to Bryan College. She wrote that she would be willing to let Eunice stay with her, and that she would act as her sponsor while she was at the college. As a result of this, Eunice was accepted by the college, and the Lord provided all her travel expenses and pocket money for the United States.

Bryan College offers only a two-year pre-nursing course and so, during the year 1981–82, we were faced again with the problem of where she could finish her nursing course and how her expenses could be met. We could not help her much out of the personal allowance we received from OMF, because we also had a 19-year-old son with us at this time. But with God nothing is impossible, so we took this matter to the Lord in prayer and Eunice applied for financial aid to several nursing schools in America. Again the Lord, in His own time, opened a way for her to go to a Mennonite college in Virginia, where she was given a full tuition scholarship and had only to take care of her board and lodging. We praise the Lord for this miraculous provi-

sion and can truly say, "Great is Thy faithfulness, O
Lord."

(MARCELO & NENO MAGHIRANG)

DAY BY DAY

Humanly speaking, it is not an easy matter for missionary parents to educate their children on the field. God has given us three children and, because we felt that the Lord wanted us to be a witness as a family unit, Alma and I decided to keep our children at home for primary education instead of sending them to Chefoo School. We sent the twin boys, David and Jonathan, to a local Chinese school in Singapore for four years, and then to a Chinese school in Taipei. Our daughter Robyn also went to Chinese school and finished her Chinese primary education in June 1983. Local school fees were relatively low so we seldom felt an urgent need for concerted prayer in respect of their tuition.

However, when the twins started their secondary education at Morrison Academy in Taichung, Taiwan, we were suddenly faced with having to pay several thousand dollars for their tuition and transportation. The OMF Secondary School Fund provided for about half of our need, and the rest of the money was supplied in wonderful ways through prayer. During our daily family devotions we prayed with the children about this, and learned two lessons through this experience. God supplied the rest of the needed funds through our relatives and friends, and the children learned valuable lessons about God's faithfulness to supply.

One night we were praying for US$200 for some educational need, and a few minutes later we found in our mailbox a cheque for US$220 from our church in Hawaii. It had been their Christmas gift, sent several weeks late, but in time to remind us that God is able to supply when we follow His will to trust Him for the seemingly impossible. At another time the twins had already been in school for two weeks before we heard that funds were available. During those two weeks we could have questioned the Lord's timing, or wondered if we should put the twins back into Chinese school or send them off to Faith Academy in the Philippines. However, we just asked Morrison Academy for an extension of the deadline to pay, and when the money did come in, we were very thankful.

In the school year 1983–84, Robyn started her studies at Morrison with the boys, which meant additional financial needs for their tuition. This was another test of faith. We continued to pray as a family for this need, and registered them without funds in hand, as we knew that God would supply because of His faithfulness in the past. And He did!

The real test of faith came when our two boys had to go to college in America in 1985. It seemed impossible to imagine paying so much money, especially over the period of four years schooling. However, we realized that God has not asked us to trust Him for the total amount at once, but for our needs each day. These we know He will supply.

(BONG & ALMA RO, FROM USA, WORK IN TAIWAN)

146

Chapter Eleven

FROM WHAT THE SAINTS LEAVE BEHIND

Godly men and women who have served God in life make sure the money they leave behind will count for God after they have died.

PROVISION THROUGH
PRAYER PARTNERS

Many years ago, when my first wife Vida was a young Christian in her teens, she knew a Christian couple whose names were Reg and Grace. Ever since those days they prayed for her, and for other missionaries whom they knew. They were pastoring a small country church in Canada, and in the course of their ministry led a woman to Christ. Her mentally unbalanced husband objected, and one night he took his gun and shot them both.

The beneficiaries from Reg and Grace's will were scattered around the world and it took two years for the lawyers to contact them all and complete the paperwork. The beneficiaries themselves then decided that all the missionaries whom Reg and Grace had prayed for should share in the legacy.

Meanwhile, Vida had had leukemia, although it had been in remission for seven years. However, while we were on holiday over Christmas 1982, she had a five-day fever. We thought it was just a virus infection and she soon recovered, but then in January the fever returned. The doctor recommended a hospital check-up, and many elaborate and expensive tests were done. It was just the day after Vida went into hospital in Bangkok, when naturally we were feeling rather low, that we received US$2,000 from the estate of Reg and Grace!

Eventually we returned to Scotland where the diagnosis was made that Vida's leukemia had returned in an acute form. Before long she went to be with her Lord. It was a hard thing He asked of us, but that legacy not only met all the Bangkok hospital bills, as well as other expenses in Scotland, but also gave us assurance of His presence and enabling at a very difficult time.

(IAN MURRAY)

During my years at Moody Bible Institute one of the teachers took a special interest in me. A strong personal relationship developed, almost like a father-son relationship. He and his wife became close personal friends of mine and he became a regular committed prayer partner as I left to go out to Asia with OMF in early 1958. We corresponded regularly over the years. I saw them every furlough and I am sure he was one of my most faithful prayer supporters.

Some years ago his wife passed away and then, in October 1981, this dear friend went to be with the Lord. I felt a tremendous sense of loss. Some time later we learned that this friend and prayer supporter had made my wife Dolores and me part-beneficiaries of his insurance policy. The proceeds made it possible for us to sell our old car and buy a newer one, as well as to pay for all our daughter Debbie's wedding expenses. But this was not all. We, along with a number of others, were also included in the will of this man who had taught thousands of young people at Moody and who had taken a deep personal interest in many of them. The money from his estate came through in time to pay all our son Tom's first-year expenses at Bible College.

(BILL WILSON)

ABOUT LEGACIES

The will, drafted way back in 1919, began as follows:

"Under a solemn sense of responsibility to Almighty God, my heavenly Father, the Giver of every good and perfect gift, including all things temporal, and recognizing that I am only His steward in the matter of the means He has entrusted to my care, I now make this my last

150

Will and Testament, after much prayerful consideration, and much waiting upon God for definite guidance in its various details.

I believe that as God has kept me free from the closest of earthly ties, such as husband and children, it is therefore His purpose that I should live solely unto Him. I further believe that He would have me devote the greater part of such moneys as He has placed in my hands for the spread of the glorious Gospel of Jesus Christ, my Lord. I believe this especially because, as far as I know, my nearest relatives do not really need such estate for their personal support."

This was the will of Charlesanna Lukens Huston of the city of Philadelphia, who has long been in the presence of our Lord. Her will names many individuals and almost every well-known Christian organization in the USA, to which funds have long since been distributed. This dear lady had a very warm place in her heart for the CIM, which was named to receive $175,000 for the Lord's work in China. It was also this lady who gave the well-remembered property in Germantown, Philadelphia, to the CIM, which served as the Mission's North American headquarters for so many years.

Miss Houston's sense of stewardship is still, in the 1980s, being productive financially in respect of the OMF. Under the provisions of her will, certain funds were left in trust for her nieces, the income to be paid to each one for her lifetime. Each niece was given the power to dispose of her respective share of the principal, but in the absence of such a disposal this share was to fall into the residue of the estate. One of the nieces died in September 1982, and in her will she expressly declined to exercise her power of disposal.

151

Therefore, her share has fallen into the residue which is directed to be distributed to the CIM — now the OMF.

(USA)

Mr X, who died in November 1939, left half the residue of his estate to the CIM on the death of his wife. She survived him by 25 years, and so it was not until 1964 that we received £5,000 on account. The remainder of the estate was made up of shares in his nursery business. Attempts were made to wind up the business, but because it was in the green belt the land could not be used for building development, and no one else wished to buy it for horticultural purposes. Therefore it was agreed to distribute the shares, and we received 9,751 one pound ordinary shares in this company. It struggled on for years, only once paying a dividend. Various attempts were made to sell the shares, but there was little market for them and we held them on our books as of no value.

Suddenly in August 1981, to our great surprise, a larger horticultural organization made an offer for the entire capital at the remarkable price of £3.85 per share! We and all the other shareholders readily agreed to this, and the sale went through. Our share of the proceeds, which came to £31,687, was mailed to us on the 42nd anniversary of Mr X's death, having appreciated by more than 300% in the interim!

(UK)

Between 1972 and 1982 OMF New Zealand benefitted to the tune of over NZ$350,000 because of legacies. This amount represents 18 percent of the total giving for this period. Many who willed either money or residue from their estates were born at the turn of the century, when CIM in New Zealand was in its infancy.

One lady was a very reticent person and her donations were always anonymous. Her appearance and life-style were frugal. However, a tenth share, amounting to $7,953, was received from this single, devoted woman's estate after her death.

Sometimes we are not aware that money has been willed to OMF until the solicitor's letter arrives. One donor had been giving between $30 and $40 a year for 42 years, until in 1978 his *East Asia Millions* magazine came back stamped "Gone — no address". He apparently died four years later in an old folks' home. The initial letter from the solicitor was followed up soon after with a cryptic, "because we can find no record of a reply from you, we thought we should write again before sending you a cheque for an interim distribution of $9,000." With alacrity the oversight was rectified, and within the week the cheque had arrived.

An auctioneer was another who always gave discreetly, asking the secretary of the Mission to meet him in the city so that he could hand over cash. Following his death the munificent sum of $48,394 was received from his estate, just before Christmas and the end of the financial year.

We closed our books at the end of November 1983, and notified Singapore International Headquarters that we could release $40,000 towards our first quarter 1984 prayer goal. We had been burdened throughout the year regarding the needs of the many New Zealand missionaries home on furlough. And the $40,000 represented barely half of what we had prayed for.

The amount was due to be remitted early in December, and I kept in mind that even yet, before the Singapore Directors had to do their sums on December

7, the Lord could supply some further significant amount.

On Monday, December 5, I collected the mail, and as my eyes scanned the envelopes I noticed one which I opened expectantly. Sure enough it was a further $22,000 from a legacy, dated December 1. We intended to release this immediately to IHQ. But at about 11 a.m. Home Director John Hewlett opened another letter. He could hardly believe his eyes! One of our representatives had written: "The enclosed will come as a great surprise. The copy of the will came a few months ago, but the cheque arrived last week. Apologies for the delay in sending the cheque to you; we had mislaid the will and thought to post them together, so decided to post cheque on and send the will when we located it, but I discovered the will today in the bottom of my brief bag!" The cheque was dated November 21, and the amount was $20,000.

As a result we were able to double our quota to the field, thus sending 86.52 percent of our prayer goal for the quarter.

"This is the Lord's doing, and it is marvellous in our eyes."

(NZ)

"NOTHING IN THE MAIL TODAY!"

Don had just been to clear the post office box. There were letters, but no donations at all. As the days passed in February, his remarks on coming home began to get monotonous — we were due to send R8,000 (US$7,843) for our South African

154

workers in Asia and the overall total for the month was R3,000 (US$2,941).

We prayed earnestly each day and set aside one day for prayer and fasting. We praised the Lord for all that came in, knowing that He would assuredly answer prayer in His time, not ours. We emphasized to all our workers the need for regular prayer for their support. As they joined us in praying, our spirits lifted, as we remembered God's great faithfulness to CIM/OMF over all the years. We could not help but praise Him.

Did the money come rolling in? No, not at first, but during the year we found that there was a steady increase in donations. We realized that God was testing us. How easily we become lethargic in our praying and take for granted the supply of our needs.

We were on a deputation tour when we received news of the death of an elderly prayer partner. Mrs Lumsden was a little old Scottish lady who lived in a modest flat not far from us. As she became increasingly frail she could no longer manage to come to our flat for the monthly prayer meeting, and so we used to pop in to visit her. She had a delightful sense of humour and to the end remained vitally interested in all the missionaries from her "favourite mission".

In due course we received notification that OMF had been included in her will. Then one day Don came back from the post office with a wide grin on his face.

"Guess how much Mrs Lumsden has left us?"

"Oh, R100."

"No more than that? Try again!"

"R1,000?"

"You'll never guess. She has left us nearly R200,000! (US$196,078)"

He went on to tell me that six missions had

benefitted from her estate, each receiving the same amount. It was unbelievable! Our little Mrs Lumsden — a millionaire! As we gave thanks to the Lord we could just imagine her in heaven, a twinkle in her eye, rejoicing that her carefully-saved money was to be used for the preaching of the gospel and the building up of the Church of Jesus Christ in many places.

Amazingly, just after this, another legacy which had been due to us since 1959 was paid out. We had lost all hope of ever receiving this legacy, which we thought was for a small sum, maybe R2,000 but because of the sale of mineral rights on the property it amounted in the end to R40,000 (US$39,215). Between the two legacies OMF benefitted by nearly one quarter of a million rand.

(DON & SYLVIA HOULISTON, THEN SOUTH AFRICA HOME STAFF)

AN EIGHTY-YEAR STORY

Grace was 19 years old when she realized that the Lord Jesus had died to be her Saviour, and that God wanted her to serve Him as a missionary in China. In 1903, at 30 years of age, Grace sailed for China with the CIM, and lived there for nearly forty years. Her main work was training and teaching girls.

During her early years in China, Grace met and married Dr William Sears and then became a member of the Southern Baptist Mission with him. Although she acquired step-children, her own little ones came by adoption.

One of these was Mavis, a Chinese baby abandoned because of poverty. Mavis, loving her new home, grew

156

up attending the school run by her adoptive mother. It seems that the relationship between them was warm and close because, when the widowed Mrs Sears left China years later, Mavis accompanied her to retirement in Australia, and decided to become an Australian citizen.

Mavis never forgot the debt of love she owed to Mrs Sears. The quiet Chinese girl had become a mature, dedicated adult. When Mrs Sears became ill, Mavis was the manager of the house and the nurse without whose loving care her "mother" would have died. Not until she was 88 did Mrs Grace Sears go to be with the Lord.

And Mavis? She threw herself into one project after another for the same Lord — Meals on Wheels, secretary of her church, exercising the gift of "helps", sewing, caring for children, reaching out to Chinese students and, as her last act, giving.

She had planned to go back to see the land of her birth, but instead she became ill and went on a different journey — right into the Lord's presence. Lying in hospital before she left, she said, "The Lord, He manages everything perfectly. The Lord knew I should not spend all that money to go to China."

That's how it was that OMF became the recipient of her substantial legacy. We can only bow our heads and say, "Thank you, Lord, for Grace and Mavis."

(AUSTRALIA)